Christmas in Texas

NUMBER THREE

The Clayton Wheat Williams

TEXAS ★ LIFE ★ SERIES

Major funding for this series was provided by
CLAYTON W. WILLIAMS, JR.

Christmas in Texas

ELIZABETH SILVERTHORNE

TEXAS A&M UNIVERSITY PRESS

College Station

The paper used in this book meets the
minimum requirements of the American National Standard for Permanence of Paper
for Printed Library Materials, Z39.48–1984.
Binding materials have been chosen for durability.

Library of Congress Cataloging-in-Publication Data

Silverthorne, Elizabeth, 1930–
    Christmas in Texas / Elizabeth Silverthorne. – 1st ed.
        p.   cm. – (The Clayton Wheat Williams Texas life
    series : no. 3)
    Includes bibliographical references (p.   ).
    ISBN 0-89096-446-7 (cloth); 0-89096-578-1 (pbk.)
    (alk. paper)
        1. Christmas–Texas.   2. Texas–Social life and customs.
    I. Title.   II. Series.
    GT4986.T4S55   1990
    394.2'68282'09764–dc20   90-10846
                                                    CIP

To Lloyd Lyman

WITH DEEP APPRECIATION FOR THE VISION AND
ENCOURAGEMENT THAT HELPED MAKE
THIS BOOK A REALITY

Contents

Preface   *page* ix

CHAPTERS

I.   Texas Celebrates: Christmas across Four Centuries   3
II.   Posadas, Pastores, and Piñatas: The Spanish-Mexican
      Heritage   21
III. Hardscrabble Christmas: The Frontier Heritage   33
IV.   Keeping the Faith: The African-American Heritage   51
V.   O Tannenbaum: The German Heritage   59
VI.   A Dickens of a Christmas: The Heritage from the
      British Isles   77
VII. Kolaches, Polkas, and Blessed Chalk: The Czech
      Heritage   93
VIII. Barnfests and Lutefisk: The Scandinavian Heritage   107
IX.   Le Père Noël: The French Heritage   117
X.   A Good Witch: The Italian Heritage   129
XI.   Festival of the Stars: The Polish Heritage   135
XII. Rumpliche and Noodles: The Wendish Heritage   145
XIII. A Harmonious Diversity: The Orthodox Heritage   151

Notes   159
Bibliography   165
Illustration Credits   179
Index   181

Preface

WE TEXANS have inherited a rich legacy of Christmas and New Year's traditions from many cultures and countries. Besides those represented in the following chapters, a number of others could be mentioned. For example, the Swiss brought along the custom of baking cookies with designs showing the infant Jesus in a stork's beak and the fun idea of serving fondue at parties. Chinese Texans, who consider the Lunar New Year the greatest holiday of the year since it is everybody's birthday, exchange ceremonial greetings and gifts on January 1.

Jews, representing different nationalities, have come to Texas from many countries and have settled in most of the major cities and towns of the state. They have established some of Texas' leading retail stores, including Neiman-Marcus, Sakowitz, and Zales, which supply Christmas shoppers with huge quantities of goods that are purchased in the stores or through ever-expanding mail order departments.

Rosh Hashanah, the Jewish New Year celebration, lasts for ten days. It begins on the first day of the Hebrew month Tishri, which usually falls in September. Traditionally it is a day of judgment, when the fate of each person, according to his conduct, is inscribed in the Book of Life. Jewish New Year's cards usually say, "May you be inscribed for a happy year."

Many Texas Jews exchange gifts and make charitable contributions during Hanukkah, or the Feast of Lights, which begins on the eve of the twenty-fifth day of the Hebrew month of Kislev and usually falls in December. It is celebrated for eight days. Eight candles are placed in an eight-branched candelabra called a *menorah,* and on each of the eight evenings of the festival one additional candle is lit.

As will be seen in the following chapters, the variety of gift bring-

ers in different cultural groups has a long and complicated history. Our Jolly Old Saint Nick or Santa Claus is undoubtedly the ghost of Saint Nicholas, a real man who was Bishop of Myra (the capital of Lycia, now part of Turkey) in the fourth century. Stories of the miracles he performed, both before and after his death, were handed down through oral tradition until they were recorded in an ancient manuscript called the Golden Legend, some five hundred years after his death.

One of his outstanding qualities was his generosity, and many European countries adopted the eve of his death day, December 6, as the time when he appeared in various guises to distribute gifts to good children. His evolution into the familiar roly-poly, red-clad grandfatherly American Santa is described in Chapter 4.

Just how and when the kindly Saint Nicholas acquired characteristics of being a stern, judgmental figure, or being accompanied by frightening, punishing companions is a mystery. Even today in some European countries, he is accompanied by a devilish companion, such as "Black Peter," a horrible creature with a dirty face, horns, red eyes, and clanking chains. Knecht Ruprecht, a well-known anti-Santa in several countries, evolved in some instances into a kindly gift giver. Corresponding figures are numerous and include Pelznickel (Furry Nicholas) and Ru Klaus (Rough Nicholas) as well as the Russian "Father Ice." In former times when parents were generally stricter and more demanding of their children, some misbehaving children did indeed find nothing but a lump of coal or a switch in their stockings. And some of the role-playing dark gift bringers actually administered whippings. Even today some small Santa believers can be persuaded to improve their behavior if they are reminded that he is checking on who is "naughty or nice."

For over three years I have been talking with Texans of varied ethnic backgrounds and gleaning from them their family customs and traditions connected with the Christmas season. I found a dislike for homogenized observances and a strong distaste for the way in which advertisements encourage greed in their children. There is a strong desire to mark the season through the use of meaningful, traditional symbols. A Czech woman said, "Last year we didn't put the mark of the Three Kings over our door with blessed chalk. We must do that this year." A German woman in Fredericksburg remembered that the chiming of all the church bells at midnight on Christmas Eve the year before had been neglected; this year she plans to arrange for the ringing of the *glocken* to herald the birth of Christ. There is an interest across the state in decorating trees with traditional ethnic symbols, in making ornaments instead of buying them ready-made, and in searching out recipes for traditional seasonal dishes.

In many towns and cities heritage societies, historical foundations, museums, church groups, ethnic societies, and fraternal organizations sponsor a wide variety of seasonal events that preserve Texas' rich heritage of Christmas traditions. Some enduring examples are the annual presentations of Las Posadas and Los Pastores in San Antonio, Christmas at Old Fort Concho in San Angelo, Dickens on the Strand in Galveston, the Lutefisk Festival at Cranfills Gap, and the Cowboys' Christmas Ball at Anson.

A few of the many people who have helped me in my search for the ethnic roots of Christmas and New Year's traditions in Texas are listed here. As always Ralph Elder and the staff of the Barker Texas History Center supplied invaluable aid in using their archives, as did Al Loman, research associate at the University of Texas Institute of Texan Cultures at San Antonio, and the Institute's library assistants, Clare Bass and Grace White. David Murrah supplied information on pioneer Christmases from the Southwest Collection at Texas Tech University. Diana

Blue, librarian at the Anson Public Library, furnished information on the Cowboys' Christmas Ball. Shay Bennett, public services librarian at the Abilene Public Library, supplied helpful material, as did librarians Jimmet Lawrence at Lamar University in Port Arthur and Mary Lou Featherston of the Port Arthur Library. Mrs. Eugene Boudoin of the Gold Triangle Cajun Association helped me with French customs. Mrs. Paul Buchanan of Mission gave me useful information on poinsettias. The Reverend John B. Culver, minister of Bethany Congregational Church in San Antonio, supplied valuable information on German Christmas customs.

Many librarians and curators have been of great assistance, including those at the Texas State Library, the DRT Library at the Alamo, the Austin History Center, the Temple Public Library, the Belton Public Library, and the Sophienburg Memorial Museum and Archives in New Braunfels. Ellen Murry, curator of education at the Star of the Republic Museum at Washington, shared her research on the subject of Christmas and New Year's in Texas. And Claire Kuehn of the Panhandle-Plains Historical Museum in Canyon sent me useful material.

I owe special thanks to Liz Carpenter, who generously shared material from her personal files. Kevin Ladd, director of the Wallisville Heritage Park, has encouraged and abetted my project from the beginning. My good friend, Thelma Fletcher, has as always been a staunch and knowledgeable supporter.

Edith Giles of Hillingdon Ranch rounded up information on ranch customs from her relatives and friends, including Elizabeth Gilliat, who graciously reviewed her family customs in a lengthy telephone interview and in correspondence.

Calvin Chervenka shared his personal files and his expertise on Czech culture, in addition to giving me valuable leads in locating material. Thelma Bartosh, curator of the SPJST Museum in Temple, has also given me valuable assistance with the Czech chapter. Leah Stimeska and Mildred and Emil Naizer of Granger have also been helpful in supplying information on Czech customs.

The Timmermann sisters of Geronimo hospitably entertained me in their historic home with a delicious meal complete with their famous Christmas cookies. They also shared valuable information and pictures.

In Gruene, Mrs. Herbert Acker showed me around her home, which was the site of the Ervendberg Orphanage.

In Fredericksburg, Helen Weirick and Hans E. Bergner talked with me in the Vereins Kirche Museum about German customs, and Dorothy Peterson, librarian at the Pioneer Library, helped me locate material on German customs. Donald Bauer, owner of the Fredericksburg Toy Museum, talked with me and lent me material from his private collection.

Lynne Hardy, library director of the Castroville Public Library, arranged for me to use oral history tapes and other material relating to Alsatian traditions.

Pauline Alpha of Dallas lent me her personal material on Wends and helped me locate other sources. Barbara Hilscher, curator at the Wendish Heritage Museum in Serbin, was very helpful in supplying material on Wendish customs.

Barbara Epley of Cranfills Gap told me the history of the Norwegian Lutefisk Festival and supplied other helpful material.

Sister Helen Widacki, Felician Sisters, St. Mary Convent, in Panna Maria graciously helped me with information on Polish traditions.

John Neilson, historian at National Historic Landmark at Fort Concho, ably assisted me in collecting material on Christmases past and present at the fort, and Susan Lane, public relations director at Fort Concho, also supplied material. Mary Williams, park ranger historian at Fort Davis National Historic Site, and the Fort Davis staff gave me valuable assistance.

Lois Douglas, chair of the French Legation Committee of the Daughters of the Republic of Texas, supplied pictures and furnished material on the French Legation of Austin.

I am indebted to the Reverend Father Evangelos S. Pepps, pastor of Saint Nicholas Orthodox Church in Waco, and to his wife Susan Pepps, presbytera of the church, for providing me with valuable information on the Orthodox Church.

I am grateful to my friends Marguerite Calvert, Charlotte Andre, Mary Farrell, Esther L. Bray, Barbara Harper, Lydia Santiago, Jack Knox, and Jacie Simmons, who have all been helpful in special ways.

The Christmas cards used to illustrate this book add a nostalgic

note and, where possible, an ethnic touch. The publishers and I gratefully acknowledge the assistance we received in gathering them. In addition to those already mentioned, we would like to thank Mary El-
Beheri, Solveig Herndon, Doris Hiebert, Wayne A. Rohne, and Mr.
and Mrs. A. L. Short.

For many years I have been collecting recipes. Many of them have
come from friends I met while living abroad and traveling in foreign
countries. Unfortunately I do not have the names of all these friends.
Recipes without sources are from my own files. Some of the recipes
have been slightly altered for the sake of consistency throughout the
book. My sincere thanks goes to them and to all my unnamed friends
who have given me suggestions, helped me find material, and wished
me well along the way.

Christmas in Texas

Just a little line to say;
Happy be your Christmasday,
Heaps of presents, lots of fun,
Mirth and joy for everyone.

Texas Celebrates:

CHRISTMAS ACROSS FOUR CENTURIES

Spanish Rule

The Spanish explorers who pushed into Texas and took possession of the land in the name of their king were of the Catholic faith, and their celebrations of Christmas were religious rituals recalling the literal meaning of Christmas: Christ's Mass. As early as 1599, the Texas Indians near present-day El Paso were introduced to Christmas pageantry when the ladies and nobles of Juan de Oñate's expedition enacted the journey of the Wise Men to Bethlehem and drafted some local Indians as extras to fill out the numbers.

Just over three hundred years ago, on December 24, 1683, a detachment of Spanish soldiers camped on a bluff overlooking the Rio del Norte, now known as the Rio Grande. They woke on Christmas morning in a barren land. Crossing the river on Christmas Day, their leader, Juan Domínguez de Mendoza, planted a "holy cross" on Texas soil and said a mass.

Three years later, French explorers celebrated the Christmas season in Texas, although regrettably they had to make do with water for their toasts, according to *Joutel's Journal of La Salle's Last Voyage:* "Monsieur de la Sale being recover'd of his Indisposition, Preparations were again made for his Journey; but we first kept the *Christmas* Holy-Days. The Midnight Mass was solemnly sung, and on *Twelve-Day,* we cry'd, *The King drinks, (according to the custom of France)* tho' we had only Water. . . ."[1]

During the early 1700s the Spanish established missions in Texas and worked hard at converting the Indians to Christianity. Among the Apache and Lipan Indians, the Spanish priests found a miraculous similarity to Christianity. These Indians paid homage to the son of Unsen, the creator, said to have been killed stretched out on the crossed spines of a great cactus. Also, most of the tribes, even the Comanches, had Christmas-like festivals, their exact date being determined by the time of the ripening of the prickly pears. Using this compatability of beliefs, plus the Indian legend of a mystical blue lady who told them about the Christ Child, the priests found it possible to convince the Indians to join in the commemoration of Christ's birth. Indian converts were allowed to perform their own traditional *matachinas* dances (depicting the struggle between good and evil) as part of the Christmas observance. Then they were given refreshments including wine. Franciscan friars dramatized the nativity for the Indians using Masses, processions, feasts, and festivals.

In 1810 Mexico began its revolt against Spain, and the threat of violent outbreaks hung over Texas. Prior to the holidays in San Antonio, Gov. Manuel María de Salcedo issued a proclamation designed to ensure a peaceful celebration. Bazaar booths and bull rings were to be located only in the plaza selected by the Feast Day Committee, and all games had to be sanctioned. Those caught drunk or disturbing the peace were to be arrested. The celebrations could only take place between vespers and the sound of taps from the parish church. After that signal everyone was to leave the streets.

The future of Texas was influenced by a chance happening during Christmas week of 1820. When Moses Austin arrived in San Antonio to present a plan to Governor Martínez for bringing three hundred Anglo-American families to Texas, his hopes were dashed because the governor refused the request and ordered Austin out of the province. Fortunately, Austin happened to meet an old friend, Baron de Bastrop, in the main plaza, and through Bastrop's intercession the decision was reversed. So important was this chance encounter to Texas that a statue has been erected to mark the site near the Spanish Governor's Palace in San Antonio.

Mexican Rule: 1821–36

After Mexico won its independence from Spain in 1821, the trickle of Anglo-Americans into Texas became a steady stream. Though survival was their main concern, they were aware of the Christmas season and when possible held religious observances. By the early 1830s they were having community parties, but for most of them there was little cheer to be had. Nevertheless, these newcomers gave Texas geography a Yuletide touch. Seven towns were given the name Bethlehem. On New Year's Day of 1821, some of Stephen F. Austin's Old Three Hundred camped by a creek that rises in east central Washington County and named it New Year Creek. Another group of the Old Three Hundred spent an uncomfortable day on December 25, 1821, camped by a creek in Limstone County, which they named Christmas Creek. Other unknown travelers named the Christmas Mountains of the Big Bend area in Brewster County. In 1826 a group of Fredonians,[2] returning to Nacogdoches after their aborted rebellion, stopped by a stream in eastern San Augustine County. After imbibing eggnog in honor of the season, they christened the stream Egg-Nog Branch.

One of the grimmest Christmas experiences recorded for 1821 involved a brave woman camped on desolate Bolivar Point. Here the twenty-three-year-old wife of adventurer Dr. James Long kept a lonely vigil waiting for her husband to return from Goliad. For shelter, Jane Long had a ragged tent and for companionship, her five-year-old daughter, a black servant girl, and the family dog, Galveston. Four days before Christmas, Jane Long gave birth to a baby girl. In addition to facing starvation and freezing weather, the little group was in danger from the Karankawa Indians in the area and from hungry predators, such as a full-grown bear recently seen in their area. But they persevered through that terrible Christmas and for six more months until help came. Jane Long lived to be called the Mother of Texas.

Other immigrants, arriving in the vicinity of Matagorda on Christmas Day, had a meager dinner, for which they were duly thankful: "A gentle breeze and fair wind sprang up, and soon we were off the mouth of the Colorado, and within about two miles of Matagorda, which then contained two families, who had lately moved down and commenced a settlement. The next day Mr. Wrightman and another went to the settlement, and returned with the present of a Christmas dinner, which consisted of some hominy, beat in a wooden mortar, and fresh milk, which were gratefully received and promptly dispatched."[3]

Since Protestant churches could not be organized in Texas under Mexican law, Christmas celebrations in early Texas were in the Catholic tradition—except for a few clandestine Protestant services. But Daniel Parker, a Texas immigrant, found a loophole in the law. Returning to his native Illinois, he started a congregation of thirty-six Protestants. Then he moved the group to Bastrop County, where they held the first legal Protestant Christmas service in Texas in 1834.

A description of a miserable Christmas Day that same Yule illustrates the difficulty of transportation in 1834: "Father shipped fifty nine bales of cotton down the Brassos River, on 2 large canoes maid out of 2 large cotton wood trees, with a platform on them. James McCoy, & Dutchman, Pa & myself, we started on Christmas morning 1834, got down the river by Mr. Henry Jones, & our boat run on a snag, & turnedover. We got wet & colde, & we had no way to git off. We hoop & hollowed & one of Mr. Jones men came to bank. He got a skift & came to us, & took us of[f], & we cut the cotton loose & floated it a shore."[4]

Stephen F. Austin had reason to remember Christmas of 1834 with pleasure, for on that day he was finally released from prison in Mexico City, after more than ten months of confinement awaiting trial on charges of plotting to separate Texas from Mexico.

By December, 1835, the Texas colonists had revolted and expelled the Mexican armed forces from the Anglo-American region. On Christmas Day of that year, many Texans were too involved with independence to celebrate the season. Among these was Gen. Sam Houston, newly elected commander of the Texas army, who spent the day setting up his headquarters at Washington-on-the-Brazos.

James W. Fannin, Jr., was also carrying out duties for the Provisional Government. As a recruiting officer, he welcomed on Christmas Day a battalion from Georgia, which had come to help Texas in the fight. William Barret Travis, a San Felipe lawyer, received a special present from the Provisional Government making him a lieutenant colonel on Christmas Day.

That same day a number of towns in Texas held special meetings to draw up resolutions arguing that the time had come for Texas to declare total and absolute independence from Mexico.

The Republic: 1836–45

By the next Christmas, independence was a fact, and for almost a decade Texas would exist as a Republic—very proud and very poor. But the citizens were free to celebrate the Christmas season with any kind of religious or secular ceremony they desired. During the years that

Texas was a nation, Christmas took on a more secular tone, although the churches continued to hold traditional services. Full of exuberance and high expectations, Texans celebrated the season with zest. Festivities lasted from Christmas Eve through New Year's Day, with rounds of dinners, dances (almost always termed balls), and parties. Many of the traditions taken for granted today had yet to be established. Only a few German immigrants had Christmas trees in their homes, and Santa Claus and his reindeer were not yet well known.

On December 25, 1836, Sam Houston, by then a popular hero, informed his audience at Washington-on-the-Brazos that their enemy, Santa Anna, was spending the holidays in Washington, D.C., as a compulsory guest of the United States. Although he was not noted for practicing temperance at that time, Houston declared that "only by continued sobriety and endeavor can a worthy Republic be formed." A huge party followed the speech, with free-flowing eggnog and a dance that lasted well into the night.

During that Christmas week of 1836, Stephen F. Austin was performing his last service for Texas, writing a paper for President Andrew Jackson setting out the reasons the United States should recognize Texas' independence from Mexico. Working in a poorly heated shack in chilly weather in spite of having a bad cold, he developed pneumonia and died on December 27.

Christmastime in 1837 was dominated by rumors that Mexican troops were on the Texas border, preparing to reinvade the Republic. The indomitable Mary Austin Holley, who was visiting in Houston, described the preparations to her daughter:

> That night (Christmas Eve) came an express making it [the Mexican invasion attempt] certain. From that time, commenced warlike preparations—all was business and bustle. The army disbanded—the militia to organize. Meetings were called, money—$2000 to $3000—subscribed & men enrolled (600 in one day) all was excitement. From Mrs Allens gallery we could overlook the whole town in motion like bees swarming—cluster of men in confab—a rushing to the Presidents house next door—every body in movement. Nobody was afraid, but every body was busy.[5]

There was not much eggnog that Christmas, she noted, as eggs were fifty cents each, and she had heard of a dozen selling for thirteen dollars. Lighting was also scant, for candles, too, were fifty cents each. And there was no sugar to be bought to make cookies and cakes.

Between Christmas and New Year's Day, Mary Austin Holley moved on to Brazoria. From there she reported on the New Year's Eve celebration: "Jany 1.38 – May you all be happy this bright New Years day my beloved children. We had a gay supper last night, & danced in the new year, though, being Sunday we did not dance out the old. A few young persons were in, among them 2 young gentlemen excellent singers & musicians on guitar, flute, violin, & Accordian. . . . After retiring they serenaded us with those instruments combined – & vocal solos. Very sweet musick. It lasted till near the time the birds commenced their morning concert."[6]

Although Texas had won independence from Mexico, it still had to win recognition of its status as a nation. On Christmas Day of 1840, for the first time, the French tricolor and the United States stars and stripes flew at the Texas capital, signifying that both countries had recognized the Republic of Texas. Despite the fact that money was tight and few Texians were wealthy, they celebrated the season with great hospitality, much visiting, and gatherings of families and friends. Communal dances were extremely popular, and on most occasions the liquor flowed freely.

In 1841, an Austin paper issued an invitation to attend a "congress of the rounders of the republic of Texas," which was to meet on December 25. The *Daily Bulletin* reported that among the early arrivals for the affair were members from "Screamersville, Slizzlejig County, Screw-Auger Creek, Toenail, Epidemic, Hyena Hollow, and Raccoon's Ford." One of the rules passed was that if a member was "too far gone to rise for a speech, the chair shall appoint a committee of three to hold him up." If he was unable to speak, the chair was to appoint a committee of two to speak for him, or if the gentleman was able to stand up only by holding onto chairs, one of the committee "should gesticulate for him." The paper noted that the congress was liberally supplied with "plenty of the source of hilarious vitality." Bills were passed and the "general tendency of legislation was to benefit the people a great deal, and the congress much more, a course for which there is plenty of precedent. . . ." The writer concluded that the great congress of sovereigns at Vienna "was not more magniloquent, nor half as jovial."[7]

Sometimes drunkenness led to rowdy, Halloween-like tricks. An undated newspaper clipping of the period reported with relief that organized entertainment helped civilize the celebrations somewhat: "Christmas week last year was one continual scene of mischief and drunken uproariousness all about town. Plows were perched to roost on the tops of houses. Signs changed their locations, and effigies of good and pious men were posted along the streets. This year all was peaceable, orderly, and quiet. The reason of this difference is obvious. This year the thoughts have been directed in a civil channel by parties and balls."[8]

In 1845 Ferdinand Roemer, a German visitor to Galveston, noted that on Christmas Eve the people celebrated by gathering in small, festive groups. On Christmas Day an acquaintance invited him to go to the Tremont House to have a glass of whiskey punch. "This is the national drink here. . . ." he commented.[9]

Noisemaking was considered essential to welcome Christmas and the New Year, and using gunpowder in some form was the handiest way. Thomas A. Hord remembered that in 1844 when he was six, there were no toys or playthings for the children of the pioneer families in his neighborhood. But they were determined to celebrate the day. Stealing some gunpowder from their fathers' supplies, they poured it in a hole in the ground and set it off. When the dust settled, some of them were slightly burned, but Hord reported worse injuries were inflicted by their fathers on their backsides.

As 1845 drew to a close, the citizens of the Republic of Texas eagerly awaited word that they had become a part of the United States. During that Christmas season, flags of the United States and of the Lone Star Republic were displayed amid the traditional decorations of red and green. Annexation was a late Christmas present, becoming official on December 29, and the new state went wild with public celebrations.

Antebellum Statehood: 1846–60

In the early years of statehood money was scarce, travel and transportation of goods difficult, and celebrations of the holidays often impromptu and original. As the population increased, different ethnic groups added their flavor to the season. Most of the cooking was still done in front of open fireplaces. Wood-burning stoves would not become common until late in the 1850s, and then only among the wealth-

ier families. Many of the commonly used Dutch ovens roasted wild turkeys for holiday feasting, but cabrito (roasted kid) and tamales were also featured. French immigrants drank spiced coffee, English celebrated around the wassail bowl and poured brandy sauce on plum puddings, while from the homes of German residents came a delicious aroma of aniseed cakes.

In spite of the difficulties of transportation, there were some expensive gifts to be had if one could afford them. In San Antonio Pentenreiders carried manufactured toys. Berends offered a sixteen-dollar set of Shakespeare, and Nette's, an early drugstore, carried French perfumes. The children of wealthy parents received fine china dolls, elaborate rocking horses, and expensive clothes. More usual gifts for Texas children, however, were dolls made from rags or corn shucks, handmade toy wagons, willow whistles, and socks filled with nuts, oranges, apples, and perhaps a hard-earned dime in the toe.

Christmas trees became increasingly popular as the decade progressed. In 1856 Pres. Franklin Pierce introduced a Christmas tree into the White House for the first time. Texans decorated their trees with whatever was handy: red berries, moss, mistletoe, cotton, pecans wrapped in colored cloth or paper, strings of popcorn, red peppers made into garlands, and homemade cookies and candies.

Among the upper crust of society, masque balls and confetti carnivals became the rage for Christmas celebrations. In the larger towns, three and sometimes four masque balls and elaborate soirees were held, with music provided by stringed instruments. Most of these affairs began at about eight and lasted until one or two in the morning. Date lists were taken around to the young men in advance, and each selected his date from the list. In this way each person had a date, or engagement as the newspapers of the day called them.

Washington County residents in 1856 celebrated with a Christmas ball in the spacious courthouse. The editor of the local paper reported that "Egg-nogs by the half bushel were manufactured in various parts of the town on and previous to Christmas day, and the jollification was pretty unanimous." On New Year's Day there was a parade of about forty riders on horses and mules of all shapes and sizes, "the riders masked and dressed in the most fantastic styles, and altogether forming quite a spectacle for an interior country village." The procession was accompanied by a "tolerably good" brass band, he said. On New Year's Eve there was another ball:

> To-night, again, the courthouse windows are illuminated, and quite a large party are tripping in on the "light fantastic toe," while I am alone in the upper story of a grocery, trying by the aid of a flickering lamp and a bad pen, to furnish the News with the items—a task, by the way, that is not of the easiest, for somebody below is trying to blow his brains out through a cracker horn, by the notes of which a crowd of heavy-footed o'boys are trying to beat time with such force as to shake the shingles on the roof. To-night ends the revelry.[10]

In 1858 the *San Antonio Herald* democratically wished "a happy Christmas to one and all whether Christian, Jew or Gentile, whether of one denomination or another, or of no denomination at all." The decade closed with an elaborate inaugural ball in Austin honoring newly elected Gov. Sam Houston. For the grand procession preceding the ceremonies, the horses were covered with red nets trimmed with silver buckles, tassels, and plumes.

When Robert E. Lee arrived at Fort Mason two days before Christmas in 1860, threats of secession were as ominous as the weather. Freezing rain made the holiday miserable, and so did the realization that Texas would almost certainly withdraw from the Union.

Civil War and Reconstruction: 1861–67

Christmas of 1861 found the Confederate flag waving among the seasonal decorations on public buildings and streets in Texas. During the holidays the Second Defense Act was approved, paving the way for Texas' military forces to play their part in the Civil War.

By the holiday season of 1862 the grim realities of the war were being brought home to Texas in a number of ways. On Christmas Day Mary A. Maverick wrote from San Antonio to her son Lewis at the front with Confederate troops: "Willie, Mary & Albert were up very early enquiring what Santa Claus had done for them & found it–'not much'– 3 young gentlemen of Magruder's staff helped four matrons decorate the church–it is very tastefully dressed . . . the pastor held service to a select congregation. . . . The day is obscure & misty but appears cheerful, children popping off powder."[11]

Families who could manage it packed sausage, smoked meats, woolen socks, gloves, mufflers, and great rolls of tobacco into tightly sewn packages addressed to their men on battlefields in the East, hoping that the gifts would arrive safely and find the intended receiver alive and well.

With Texas ports blockaded, all gifts were homemade and all food homegrown. Innovative cooks set themselves the challenge of producing Christmas cakes without white sugar or flour, raisins, or many other customary ingredients. Coffee was probably the thing the Texans missed most. They tried making it from parched grains, acorns, okra, sweet potatoes, and anything else they could think of, but never with much luck. Texas women, scornful of wearing clothing of lace or silk imported from the North, proudly wore homespun with Beauregard sleeves to their Christmas dances.

In Woodlawn, their stately mansion in Austin, the former governor Marshall Pease and his family used their imaginations to overcome shortages. Under the direction of his wife, Lucadia Pease, the carpets were taken up and sewed into overcoats for the slaves. Lucadia prided herself on learning to cobble and on making fancy candles. Coloring the candles she called "the great art of arts." She experimented with leaves, berries, bark, and roots of every kind plus long and short moss. Sometimes they expected one color but got another. Then "we had only to try again with hope of better luck," Lucadia wrote cheerfully. The Peases kept goats, eating the meat and using the skin for shoes. Their daughter, Julia, never forgot the Christmas of 1863:

> The Christmas tree was just a common cedar, cut by old Tom. Sprawling it certainly was, making it difficult to attach the many bundles done up in wrapping paper and home-made twine. The ladies worked for days stringing popcorn, making cornucopias and pasting on them the bright prints which had been saved for months. My mother cut out a pair of slippers from the kid skin and my sister and I embroidered them as a gift for my father. On cloth, with the aid of the governess, we did the same for my mother. Hideous things, they were, no doubt, but our patience and love redeemed all.[12]

There were pecans, peanuts, homemade candies, and small cakes to fill the cornucopias on the Peases' tree, and after the gifts were handed out, Mrs. Pease ladled out foamy eggnog for everyone, including the servants.

By Christmas of 1864, homemade clothing, food, drink, and gifts were even more essential. Gold was $5,000 a pound, flour was $600 a barrel, sugar $2 an ounce, butter $40 a pound, firecrackers $5 a pack, and real tea was worth $100 a pound. Merchants had little of anything to sell, and for what they did have they refused to take worthless Confederate money, insisting instead on gold or silver.

The holiday season of 1865 found the war finally ended and Texas occupied by Union troops. On December 21, 1865, the *Galveston News* carried advertisements from merchants who had received supplies of "candy, raisins, whiskey, tobacco, coffee and dry goods" in time for Christmas. A sad postscript on the horrors of war were advertisements for metallic artificial legs for $100 to $125, "cheaper and more long lasting than wooden legs."

The young Maj. Gen. George Armstrong Custer and his bride, Elizabeth Bacon Custer, were stationed in Austin on the grounds of the old Blind Asylum. The Custers, who liked Austin and showed it, were well received by the citizens of the town after a short time. Elizabeth Custer reported to her mother:

We had a lovely Christmas. I fared beautifully, as some of our staff had been to San Antonio, where the stores have a good many beautiful things from Mexico. Here, we had little opportunity to buy anything, but I managed to get up some trifle for each of our circle. We had a large Christmas-tree, and Autie [Custer] was Santa Claus, and handed down the presents, making side-splitting remarks as each person walked up to receive his gift. The tree was well lighted. I don't know how so many tapers were gotten together. . . . We played games, sang songs. . . . [and] danced. . . . The rooms were prettily trimmed with evergreens, and over one door a great branch of mistletoe. . . .[13]

By July Custer and his volunteers had left Austin, and a tough group of veteran regulars, the Sixth Cavalry, had replaced them. It took about six months for the icy relations between the Austinites and their unwelcome guests to begin to thaw. Late on the afternoon of Christmas Eve, 1866, the regimental band gave a concert on the grounds of the capitol for the soldiers and the citizens of Austin. The audience listened appreciatively and applauded each number politely. But when the band played "Yankee Doodle," the citizens stood in stony silence while the soldiers cheered. Then the bandmaster began passing out new sheet music to his musicians, who grinned when they saw it. Expecting some new insult, the audience waited tensely. The bandmaster rapped his stand, and the Sixth Cavalry band struck up "Dixie."

After a minute of stunned silence, someone gave a rebel yell, and the crowd erupted—shouting, tossing hats in the air, slapping backs. "Dixie" was played four times and then the band played "Home, Sweet Home." A reporter wrote: "As the concert ended and the band was dismissed, each Yankee had as many Rebs, male and female holding onto him, as could lay hands on him."[14]

By 1867, Texans were again celebrating Christmas with exuberance. The term Christmas Tree was used with quotation marks by newspapers, indicating it was still something of a novelty, but decorated trees were fast gaining popularity, and wagon loads of evergreens were brought into the main plaza in San Antonio daily during the weeks before the holiday. Stores advertised books, toys, slippers, dressing gowns, and "fancy goods" as suitable gifts. The Haight and Chambers New Orleans Colossal Circus and Menagerie pitched its tents not far from the present city hall of San Antonio. Every night during Christmas week, San Antonians filled the tents to watch acrobats perform on trapezes and on horseback. Lion tamers thrilled the crowds, but a performing baby elephant stole the show. On New Year's Eve the Orton Brothers Circus was in town, featuring a novel "Twelve-Piece Female Silver Cornet Band." Firecrackers were again affordable, and the *Herald* reported "a continual explosion of fireworks, firing of pistols, and a great deal of noise generally."

Late Nineteenth Century: 1870–1900

With the coming of the railroad, transportation was made increasingly easy, and more goods were available to choose from. The first iron horse huffed into Austin on Christmas Day, 1871, amid jubilation and celebrations. On the next Christmas Day, Texans received the gift of a railroad connection with the rest of the United States, when a wood-burning locomotive pulled a string of cars across the Red River into the new town of Denison.

Austin papers that season reflected the contrast between sacred and secular celebrations in the town. Several columns of the Austin *Daily Statesman*'s December 25 issue listed church activities. Saint Mary's held a high midnight mass. The Baptist church had a Christmas tree for the children, and the German Methodist Church had a program with speeches and recitations by its Sunday School students. In another section, under the heading, "Christmas Doings at the Saloons," the paper reported: "Most of the Austin saloons will 'make merry' in a genteel way on Christmas morning, and will treat friends and patrons to excellent egg-nog. . . . The Senate Saloon will celebrate with a raffle for turkeys along with the egg-nog." The article included a listing of the saloons with the times free eggnog would be served at each. Anyone making the rounds would indeed have had a very merry Christmas.

One of the Christmas activities available in San Antonio was a practice turkey shoot on the afternoon of December 25, near the Government Corral. It was promised that "the best shots in the county will be there."

In 1876 people had come from miles away to stare up at the glass and tinsel ornaments glittering in the light of myriads of candles on a Christmas tree in the window of a German family living over a drugstore on Main Street in Dallas. But by the late 1880s Christmas trees were all the rage. The Austin *Statesman* advised its readers: "If you can't pay two dollars for one, take a hatchet, go out in the woods and poach on somebody's forest. You *must* have a Christmas tree or there will be no Christmas."[15]

Prostitutes who lived in the red-light district of San Antonio on Matamoros and Monterrey streets shared the Christmas spirit. The San Antonio *Light* of December 24, 1886, noticed that "nearly all the bawdy houses in the city will give Christmas dinners to their 'guests' and have issued printed invitations, sending them to nearly every young man in the city."

By the last decade of the century, the custom of holding a New Year's Day open house was a well-established rite. In 1856, Lucadia Pease had written to her family back in Connecticut, "The practice of calling on New Year's Day is not observed here, tho' Ashbel Smith with his Frenchified manners gave me a call that morning. . . ."[16] But on January 2, 1895, the Austin *Statesman* reported: "The society circles of Austin were all on the move yesterday. At the various open houses there were hundreds of elegantly gowned callers." The reporter described the hospitality of individual hostesses and their tables, which were intricately decorated and heavy with fine food and plentiful champagne to wash it down. At the Governor's Mansion, New Year's Day also had become a traditional time of open house with "elegant hospitality" for the citizens.

A Dallas paper society editor write, "Many ladies make the New Year reception the occasion for brilliant display and entertain their friends with sumptuous collations."[17]

Texas has always been, and probably will always be, a land of contrasts. While the city ladies were entertaining with style and grace, cowboys celebrated the season with lusty prancing and a lot of noisy explosions. The spirit of their celebrations is caught by S. Omar Barker in "Oldtime Christmas Gallyhoot":

> Them oldtime cowboy gallyhoots was Christmas in the rough,
> For some of them ol' buckaroos was rootin'-tootin' tough,
> But punchin' cow was lonesome work, and Christmas was a chance
> To beat the "bunkhouse lonesomes" with a little prowl and prance,
> A little whoop and holler and a little panther juice,
> And all the other trimmin's of a cowpoke on the loose.
> A home-folks Christmas would have suited some—and they admit it—
> But cowboys had to take their fun wherever they could git it![18]

During the 1890s major hotels began luring people away from their home-cooked Christmas dinners by offering extravagant feasts. The Menger in San Antonio included on its Christmas menu Benwick Bay oysters, green sea turtle, baked filet of trout au gratin, prime beef with Yorkshire pudding, turkey with oyster dressing, and young pig with applesauce. By 1897, railroads were trying to lure families away from their homes for the holidays by offering Christmas excursion fares to Old Mexico and to the North and Southeast.

By the turn of the century, many groups had established traditional annual activities. The Beethoven Männerchor gave an elaborate choral program, followed by a dance. The San Antonio German Club held yearly Christmas cotillions. The Jewish members of the community observed Hanukkah, and the Italians, Poles, and French each celebrated the season with traditional rituals.

The less fortunate were not forgotten. Christmas boxes were handed out, and in 1899 a thousand meals were served to the "sick and poor" in the Orinski Building on Military Plaza in San Antonio. In Austin, the Charles Lundbergs, owners of the largest bakery in the city, established an annual custom of sending a big Christmas dinner to those unlucky enough to be spending Christmas in the county jail.

As the century ended, two thousand people attended the traditional midnight mass at San Fernando Cathedral. The church was decorated with roses and evergreens, and it was reported in the papers that "the glare of electric lights lent a pretty effect." It had been a long time since the first Christmas mass held by lonely Spanish soldiers on Texas soil by the light of the stars and the moon.

The Twentieth Century

In 1914 Austin had its first outdoor municipal Christmas tree, which was set up at the entrance of the capitol. Bands, combined adult choirs from different churches, and a thousand school children provided music. "The mightiest cedar in Travis County" was magnificently illuminated with hundreds of small lights and a glowing star at its top. This was the beginning of the custom for cities, towns, and villages of all sizes in Texas to have a ceremonial lighting of a community tree.

That same year the Rotary Club sponsored a Big Brothers program, collecting and distributing clothing, fuel, bedding, groceries, and toys to five hundred families (about two thousand people). The Salvation Army planned a menu to feed three hundred people. There was a municipal fireworks display. And there were dances, dinners, and innumerable parties for what the *American-Statesman* called "Austin's greatest of all great Christmases."

Since 1914 similar patterns of celebrations have been held throughout the state with only slight curtailments during World Wars I and II and during the Great Depression.

Just before Christmas in 1927, Cisco was the scene of a crime that became a West Texas legend. A. C. Greene has written a book about *The Santa Claus Bank Robbery.* The gang's leader wore a Santa Claus disguise because he was known in Cisco. But he didn't figure on having children follow him into the bank. The inept robbers got into a shooting match with trigger-happy citizens of the town, the getaway car ran out of gas because they forgot to fill the tank, and in switching to a second car, they left all the loot behind. The comedy of errors turned into a tragedy as several people were killed. After a grueling manhunt, one of the robbers died of gunshot wounds, one died in the electric chair, and one went to prison. Santa himself was lynched by an Eastland mob in a grotesque scene. His family took his body to Fort Worth for burial, but the services had to be delayed because of a passing parade, signaling the beginning of the Christmas season two years after the robbery. Ironically, the parade was led by a Santa Claus figure.

From the huge star on Franklin Mountain in El Paso to the light display on the old courthouse in Marshall, from the harbor lights at Corpus Christi to the lights festooning oil derricks in Kilgore, Texans light up the season. Displays are as new as the one at the Queen of Vietnamese Martyrs Catholic Church in Port Arthur and as old as the *luminarias* in San Antonio lighting the way of the ancient *Posada* processions. Newspapers publish information on where to go to see the most outstanding displays of lights. But amid all the glitter, in the midst of all the hustle and bustle that goes along with modern celebrations of the season, many feel a void, a need for something more.

For many Texans Christmas is a year-round business, especially for those responsible for Christmas fairs and markets, parades, and other public celebrations. Christmas bazaars are held long before Thanksgiving in many Texas towns, and municipal light displays begin earlier each year. Under the influence of radio and television, celebrations have become more homogenized and commercialized. In stores and in homes the pressure is on to put up Christmas trees and decorations earlier each year. Christmas carols blasting continually in malls have a numbing effect on the mind and spirit. A few years ago Henderson Shuffler wrote: "Strange, primitive Christmases, these old-time Texans had . . . not at all like our modern holidays, in which we keep a running statewide count of the number of liquored-up citizens who did themselves and others in with auto mishaps, or kept the holy season with murder, mayhem and other fatal types of celebrations. . . . Christmas in early Texas just wasn't up to our modern standards—the Lord be praised![19]

It takes some effort in the late twentieth century to remember "the reason for the season," as the plastic buttons say. But an encouraging note is the conscious and enthusiastic determination of different groups across the state to preserve the traditions of Christmas with religious ceremonies and meaningful symbols, music, food, and customs that have been imported to Texas across four centuries.

Posadas, Pastores, and Piñatas:

THE SPANISH-MEXICAN HERITAGE

¡Feliz Navidad!   Hispanic children whose families observe traditional Christmas customs are lucky. Pancho Claus gives them presents on December 25, and the Three Kings bring them gifts on January 6. They enjoy turkey and tamales, buñuelos and brownies, fiestas and fandangos and fireworks, and Masses with maria-chi bands. They play with new electronic toys, but scream with delight as they participate in the breaking of the piñata—a game brought to Mexico by the Spanish explorers over four hundred years ago. The Bless-ing of the Animals in San Antonio is a good example of the updating of a very old Christmas ritual brought to Texas from Mexico. A Fran-ciscan friar travels from Mission San José to historic Market Square, where he blesses a variety of pets—from dogs and cats to snakes and even some stuffed animals. The mayor proclaims the day "Pet Aware-ness Day," and anti–animal abuse organizations in the city participate.

For over three hundred years (1528–1836), Mexico and the province of Texas were closely linked. Our Spanish-Mexican heritage has influ-enced our laws and language, our legends and lore and has given us some of our most colorful holiday customs. Spanish padres in the early Texas missions allowed their Indian converts to perform their own tra-ditional dances on Christmas Eve and celebrated the occasion with wine. The padres also provided spiritual entertainment for the converts with processions, plays, feasts, and festivals intended to dramatize the mean-ing of the nativity and to convey the Christian idea of joy over the birth of the Savior.

There is an enduring legend of a miracle that happened at an early Christmas celebration at the Mission San Antonio de Valero, now known as the Alamo. The mission was established by the venerable Fray Antonio Margil, the first *padre presidente* of Texas missions. At Christmastime in 1719, the missionaries set up a realistic nativity scene, using native mosses and foliage, and invited the Indian children to bring gifts for the Christ Child in the manger.

Some brought strings of beads and animal claws, brightly colored feathers and bits of cloth, furs of small animals, and painted horns of buffalo. But one small Indian boy, Shavano, whose family was very poor, had nothing to give the Infant. Finding Shavano crying bitterly, Father Margil comforted him and went with him in search of a gift. Finally they came upon a little vine with green berries and leaves, which they dug up and planted in a clay pot. Although Shavano was not satisfied with his spindly offering, he presented it, asking the Christ Child to accept it and make it beautiful.

The next morning, the story goes, Shavano heard people crying, "¡Milagro! ¡Milagro!" (Miracle! Miracle!). Hurrying to the manger scene, he found that the vine had grown and twined itself around the crèche. Its leaves had become a glistening dark green, and the berries had turned bright red, making it the most beautiful of all the gifts around the manger. The vine still grows wild around San Antonio, and at Christmastime its berries are scarlet and its leaves bright green. It has a long scientific name, but the natives call it the Margil vine in honor of Padre Margil, who witnessed the miracle of that early Christmas at the Alamo.

The poinsettia, another colorful Christmas plant, came to Texas and to the United States from Mexico because of politics connected with Texas. Joel R. Poinsett, the first American minister to Mexico, was in that country during the Christmas season of 1828, trying to purchase the territory of Texas for the United States. A knowledgeable botany buff, Poinsett was charmed by the plant the Aztecs called *cuitlaxochitz*, "false flower," and the Mexicans called the flower of Christmas Eve or Mexican flame leaf. He carried cuttings of the plant back to his home in South Carolina and later sold their cuttings to a nurseryman in Philadelphia. The flower came to be called the poinsettia in his honor and soon became a popular symbol of the Christmas season. South Texas proved a fertile area for growing the colorful plant, and the town of Mission in the Rio Grande Valley is now the home of the national headquarters of the American Poinsettia Society. Each year in December the town comes alive with brilliant floral displays. In 1989 the forty-eighth annual Tropical Christmas Poinsettia Show was presented by the Mission Garden Club. Today it would be hard to imagine Christmas without poinsettias.

After Texas became a state, Mexico continued to contribute large numbers of immigrants. In 1853, an Irish nun, cloistered in the old Ursuline Convent in San Antonio, wrote a letter to her motherhouse in Ireland describing the celebration of Christmas by the San Antonio Mexicans: "Already the Mexicans have begun their preparations for 'La Noche Buena'–Christmas. As soon as night falls lamps are lighted & raised high above the houses–this is done every night till the Epiphany. This morning there was a great firing of cannon in honor of 'Our Lady's Expectations.' The great feast of the Mexicans is after Midnight Mass on Christmas morning, when they have a grand supper."[1]

Las Posadas (the inns) is one of the most beautiful traditions that has come to us through Mexico.[2] It is a reenactment of Mary and Joseph's journey to Bethlehem and their search for a room where Jesus could be born. Originally nine families took part in the novena. One family started the journey, singing carols along the candle-lit way and requesting entrance at a second home. The request was denied, but each succeeding family joined the group in the search until eight families were standing at the door of the ninth family, who granted the request for *posada*. Refreshments were served and praise and prayer offered before a manger. The ritual continued each night until Christmas Eve when all nine families had been hosts. The ninth night was a time for celebration.

Recently, Mexican-Americans in Texas have embraced the ancient custom of *posadas* with increasing enthusiasm. The best-known production is probably the *posada* that has been sponsored by the San Antonio Conservation Society for twenty-five years. It involves hundreds of participants wending their way down the River Walk from La Mansion del Rio Hotel to historic La Villita. Candles and songbooks are distributed to all who wish to join, and local choirs interspersed throughout the procession lead the singing of carols, which can be sung in Spanish or English. After being refused shelter at River Square and the Hilton Hotel, the Holy Family and their followers are welcomed at the Arneson River Theater by the archbishop. Then everyone is invited to a piñata party with folkloric dancing and refreshments of hot chocolate and cookies.

Las Posadas is also performed privately by families and neighborhood groups from December 16 through December 24. The participants are divided into pilgrims and innkeepers. The pilgrims carry lighted candles and sing carols as they walk through the streets or patios to the closed doors behind which the innkeepers wait. Joseph and the chief innkeeper sing a duet in which Joseph pleads, "Mary my wife is expecting a child. She must have shelter tonight. Let us in! Let us in!"

The innkeeper replies, "I do not trust you. Go away! Go away!"

Joseph begs for pity, but the host refuses admittance until Joseph tells him, "My wife is the Queen of Heaven / Chosen by God to deliver His Son."[3] At this, the innkeeper relents and lets them enter. An image of the Holy Infant is placed in the manger, and the pilgrims and innkeepers gather round it to sing "Las Posadas." This lullaby's first verse says:

> Thou art well content in a stable so lowly,
> Where the shepherds praise Thee as God's Son so holy.
> Go to sleep, my baby, my sweetest One,
> My Jesus dear, my fairest.[4]

In the Mexican tradition of combining reverence with festivity, it is then time for the social part of the evening, including refreshments, dancing, and the breaking of the piñata.

Piñatas, made of clay or papier-mâché, come in all shapes and sizes. Often they are in animal forms. Traditional stars, lambs, and crosses are still popular, but next to them can be found satellites and Santa Clauses. Covered with brightly colored tissue paper and stuffed with candy, small toys, and good luck charms, a piñata is hung from the ceiling with ropes attached so it can be hauled up and down. A blindfolded player tries to hit the piñata with a wooden stick while the other players twitch the ropes, making it jerk out of reach, as they urge on the blindly swinging player with shouts of conflicting advice. Finally someone connects with a blow that smashes the piñata. Its contents shower down, and there is a wild scramble to gather up the goodies.

La Fiesta de las Luminarias (the Festival of Lights) is a Mexican-American tradition that dates back to sixteenth-century Spain. It, too, began as a religious ritual with the lights symbolically illuminating the way for Mary and Joseph as they traveled to Bethlehem. In another interpretation, the lights guided the way for the Magi. Originally the light came from small bonfires, but through the centuries these evolved into *luminarias,* paper bags weighted with sand and holding small candles.[5] Today the romantic paper bag *luminarias* are sometimes replaced by more convenient electric bulbs in ceramic containers shaped like paper bags. Many cities, towns, and villages in Texas have taken up the lovely custom of outlining walks, streets, walls, and buildings with *luminarias.* The thousands of candles along the River Walk in San Antonio plus the thousands of tiny lights in the trees make it an enchanting scene during the Christmas season.

A few Mexican-American families continue the custom of hanging a kerosene lamp on their front porches during the holidays or turning on a small red electric bulb. Originally the lamps represented the star over Bethlehem when Christ was born. They were a sign of invitation to carolers and friends to enter the homes for refreshments of hot chocolate, tamales, and buñuelos and to view the family *nacimiento*, or manger scene.

In Catholic families of Mexican heritage, the *nacimiento* is usually given more importance than the Christmas tree. Each *nacimiento* is different, and many are personalized with individual creative touches. Simple *nacimientos* may consist only of images of Joseph, Mary, and the Christ Child, with perhaps a donkey and a sheep to indicate the stable. More detailed scenes may include a wide sweep of country around Bethlehem with an elaborate layout of hills, mountains, roads, and towns. The three Wise Men, angels, shepherds with their sheep, and other animals may be displayed in addition to the figures of the Holy Family.

The Yanez family home in Temple features a *nacimiento* that reaches from floor to ceiling. Built of evergreens, theirs is adorned with hundreds of ornaments, tinsel, wreaths, and figures portraying both secular and religious elements of the season. There is a devil (to represent the evils of the world), a Father Time, the Virgin Mary traveling to Bethlehem, hens (to herald a new day), a cactus, and a Santa complete with sleigh and reindeer.

According to a family's means, the figures may be of fine china, clay, wood, plaster, plastic, cardboard, or paper. But even the humblest scene may have a Christ Child made of exquisite porcelain. The manger in the *nacimiento* remains empty until midnight of Christmas Eve when the baby is "born." And the scene remains in place until the three Magi reach it on January 6 to present their gifts to the Holy Infant. This is the climax of the holiday season and the traditional gift-giving day for Mexican families. In earlier days the children would have written letters to "Los Reyes Magos" telling them what gifts they would like to receive. And on the eve of January 6, they would put out their shoes filled with straw for the camels of the Three Kings. During the night the parents would remove the straw and substitute their gifts. When Texas families of Mexican heritage put up Christmas trees in addition to *nacimientos,* the decorations are often gaily painted tin angels, stars and bright paper flowers, straw figures and white birds with candlewax bodies and paper wings. A new decorating trend that has come to Texas from Mexico via New Mexico is the use of red peppers—real, plastic, or ceramic.

Another popular tradition among Mexican Texans is the ancient *Los Pastores* (The Shepherds), a drama probably derived from a cycle of medieval mystery plays, which draws audiences of many backgrounds. In the Old World the play passed from church control into the hands of the folk, who added comic scenes and some irreverent characters. Brought to New Spain by conquistadors, the play acquired Indian elements and modern insertions. Although it was presented at Mission San José as early as 1776, the lines were taught to the actors by rote, and the play was not codified and printed until 1940, when the Reverend Carmelo Tranchese, priest at Our Lady of Guadalupe Church in San Antonio, published it in English and Spanish from handwritten notes brought from Mexico in the early 1900s.

The best-known version is the one sponsored annually by the Conservation Society of San Antonio and performed by the Guadalupe Church players at Mission San José. This outdoor presentation has been a joint collaboration at the mission since 1945, when the Society members joined forces with the parishioners of Our Lady of Guadalupe to bring the drama to the community. Members of the audience bring folding chairs and blankets and may purchase refreshments of coffee, hot chocolate, spiced cider, tamales, and chili from food booths on the grounds. As the moon begins to climb overhead, they watch the unfolding of the old, old story against the background of the finest mission church built by the Franciscan friars.

Authorities have estimated that there are upwards of a hundred performances of the play each year in the San Antonio area alone and uncounted numbers of performances in other cities with substantial Mexican-American populations. When all of the songs (which are simple chanted hymns), dialogue, and characters are included, the play can run very long indeed. There are stories of performances lasting from dusk to dawn, although three to four hours is more common. Performances include time out for the players to have a meal, which is written into the script. The "tourist" version is also usually shorter.

Whatever version is used, the basic plot is simple and revolves around the shepherds, who are trying to get to Bethlehem, and the evil forces led by Satan, which are trying to stop them. The twenty-four characters have to learn long speeches, songs in minor keys, solos, and high-flown choruses. Traditionally the parts are memorized and handed down from father to son in the manner of the Passion Play of Oberammergau. *Los Pastores* is an act of faith and of spiritual satisfaction for the audience as well as the players. No admission is charged, and the players not only are not paid, but also are expected to furnish their own costumes and props. The fourteen herdsmen take especial pride in their tall staffs, which are decorated with paper flowers, bells, and birds.

Among the many anachronisms in the play is the Hermit, who comes on stage wearing a Franciscan habit and carrying a cross. A favorite of the audience is invariably the lazy shepherd called Bartolo. Interested only in sleeping and eating, he suggests that if the Christ Child cannot be brought to him, the others can carry him to Bethlehem on a mattress so he can present a tamale to the Child as his gift. In some versions the shepherds are threatened by an American Indian in buckskin and feathered headdress as well as by traditional devils in hideous costumes. There are also Indian dancers who perform traditional *matachinas* dances. But the audiences are not concerned with the logic of the performance. For them the play is a treasured religious artifact, and many of them know nearly every one of the five thousand or so lines in it. As good and evil battle back and forth, they groan or exult with the players.

Finally Saint Michael, a little boy, faces the main devil and strikes him down. The shepherds make their way to Bethlehem and kneel to present their gifts. Members of the audience follow them to the manger to join in worshiping the Holy Family. The shepherds sing their farewell, "Adiós, niño chiquitito . . . adiós, adiós, adiós, Jesúsito. . . ." Much of the story of *Los Pastores* unfolds in the music, which has been recorded and preserved at the Barker Texas History Center at the University of Texas. The play is performed from December 24 through February 2 at Mission San José, but traditionally performances may be given from December 15 on into March.

For Mexican Texans feasting is an important part of the fiestas connected with Christmas. *Posole* is lime-treated hominy, and it is also the name of a popular holiday dish that combines hominy, pork, and chicken with chili powder and green chilis. Served in bowls with garnishes of shredded lettuce, lime wedges, scallions, and radishes, it is a meal in itself. Tamales star on holiday menus. In addition to the more usual pork, beef, and chicken fillings, special tamales for the festivities may have fruit centers or centers of nuts and seeds.

Cinnamon enhances traditional Mexican Christmas foods, such as turkey mole and crispy *buñuelo* fritters.

Mole de Guajolote
(TURKEY WITH MOLE SAUCE)
Pan American World Airways

6–8 lb. turkey, cut in serving pieces	½ cup almonds
2 t. salt	8 tomatoes
½ cup olive oil	½ t. cinnamon
3 green peppers	¼ t. pepper
2 T. sesame seeds	2 T. chili powder
6 cloves garlic	2 oz. unsweetened chocolate,
1 slice dry white toast	grated

Cook turkey pieces in water to cover, together with 1 teaspoon salt. Cook until almost tender, about 1½ hours. Drain, reserving 2 cups stock. Dry turkey. Heat ¼ cup olive oil in a frying pan. Add turkey and brown well on all sides. Remove turkey, and place in a casserole. Grind together green peppers, sesame seeds, garlic, toast, almonds, and tomatoes. Add cinnamon, remaining salt, pepper, chili powder, and chocolate, and mix well. Heat remaining oil, and add mixture. Cook over low heat for 5 minutes, stirring constantly. Place casserole over low heat and pour stock over turkey. Spread chocolate mixture over turkey. Cover, and cook for 2 hours. Stir occasionally. Serve hot with boiled rice, and pour sauce over rice. Makes 6–8 servings.

The aroma and taste of fresh *buñuelos* are part of the Christmas memories of Mexican Texans of all ages. Sometimes called Mexican doughnuts, *buñuelos* may be either puffy or flattened depending on how the dough is handled and on how much baking power is used.

Buñuelos

¾ cup milk
4 T. butter
1 T. aniseed, slightly crushed
1 t. salt
2 beaten eggs

3 cups all-purpose flour
1 t. baking powder
cooking oil for deep-fat frying
½ cup sugar
1 t. ground cinnamon

In small saucepan, heat milk, butter, aniseed, and salt to boiling. Cool to room temperature. Stir in beaten eggs. In mixing bowl, stir together flour and baking powder. Add egg mixture. Mix well.

Turn dough out onto lightly floured surface. Knead till smooth, 2 or 3 minutes. Divide, and shape dough into 20 balls. Cover; let rest 10 minutes. Roll out each ball into 4-inch circle. (For flatter buñuelos, allow rolled dough to stand, uncovered at room temperature for 20 minutes, turning after 10 minutes to allow surface to dry slightly.) Fry, one at a time, in deep hot fat (375°) for 4 minutes or till golden brown, turning once. Keep remaining circles of dough covered. Drain on paper towels. Combine sugar and cinnamon in plastic bag. Gently shake warm buñuelos, one at a time, in sugar mixture.

It is generally agreed that *buñuelos* taste best when accompanied by Mexican hot chocolate. Many large supermarkets carry Mexican chocolate, which comes in squares or rounds already sweetened and flavored with cinnamon. It can also be purchased in Mexican specialty stores. A square or round of chocolate is dissolved in a cup of hot milk for each serving. After the chocolate has melted, the mixture is poured into a pitcher and beaten vigorously with a *molinillo* (a wooden beater that is twirled between the hands) until the chocolate is frothy. The hot chocolate drink is sometimes thickened with corn meal to make a drink called *champurrado*.

A favorite candy to offer guests during the holidays is *leche quemada* (burned milk candy), a tasty caramel-flavored sweet.

Leche Quemada

I qt. milk
2 cups sugar

⅛ t. cream of tartar
pecan halves

Place milk, sugar, and cream of tartar in a saucepan. Stir to dissolve. Cook over low heat about I hour or until mixture begins to thicken. Stir occasionally at first, and toward end of time stir constantly. Cook to soft ball stage or 232° on candy thermometer. Remove from heat. Pour into 9×9×2-inch cake pan lined with wax paper, and let cool. Cut into small squares. Press a pecan half into each square.

Attending *Misa de Gallo,* the mass of the cock or midnight mass, on Christmas Eve is a time-honored Hispanic custom. Before the turn of the century, the observance seems to have gotten out of hand. Between 1875 and 1881 the Christmas Eve midnight mass was suspended in San Antonio by edict of the Roman Catholic bishop. The San Antonio *Express* explained the problem: "Persons stay up, ramble about the streets and get drunk and noisy and then go to the Midnight Masses, rendering them instead of occasions of quiet holy joy, scenes of disorder and unrighteous conduct."[7] During the years of the ban, Christmas masses were scheduled at 6 A.M., when it was hoped, the paper reported, that "disorderly and boisterous persons, idle critics and spectators who come but to calumniate, ridicule or condemn will be kept away." In 1881 when the midnight masses were restored, the *Express* issued an editorial warning: "The church is no place to smoke or be boisterous, or guilty of ungentlemanly conduct. Father Genolin feels humiliated in having to call public attention to these points, and only does so after patience and forbearance almost equal to Job."[8] Today, these masses in churches all over Texas are a high point of the Christmas season for Catholic Mexican Texans. They are festive and enlivened with mariachi music and carols sung in two languages.

Like New Yorkers, San Antonians gather in the thousands in the heart of their city to welcome in the New Year. That evening, entertainment and food booths are located throughout La Villita Historical

District. At midnight all eyes turn toward the buildings that are reminders of the city's unique history and watch as the Alamo and the Tower of the Americas are lit up by multicolored showers of sparks from exploding fireworks.

Hardscrabble Christmas:

THE FRONTIER HERITAGE

Merry Christmas! One Christmas Eve a bitter norther caught a group of wagon freighters near the Pedernales River. Their wagons were heavily loaded with salt and other goods from the Corpus Christi area, and they couldn't make it home for Christmas. Undaunted, they made camp on the frozen ground and fixed up a small cedar for their Christmas tree. Then they began hauling out what they had to donate. One brought out plugs of tobacco, another provided a jug of whiskey, and a third took a side of bacon from his wagon. Far from home, they managed to share a jolly Christmas celebration.

Their attitude is typical of the unquenchable spirit of the Anglo-Americans who poured into Texas after 1821 when it was officially opened to immigration from the United States. By sheer force of numbers these Anglo-Americans, or Anglos as they were often called, soon dominated the social, political, and economic systems of the territory, and English became the predominant language. Most of these Anglos were second- or third-generation descendants of settlers from northern and central Europe, and most of them moved into Texas from the agricultural South.

Transportation was slow and difficult; material goods were hard to come by. They lived close to nature and were largely self-sustaining. But they celebrated the holiday season with zest—drinking, dancing, singing, feasting, and making a joyful noise. Fireworks in the form of firecrackers, skyrockets, and Roman candles were not widespread in Texas until they were introduced by Chinese workers who came to build railroads after the Civil War. But the early Texans found their own ways to make noise.

Guns were a necessity on the frontier and gunpowder was readily available. Gunpowder poured into holes bored in logs or tree stumps was set off with a piece of punk. Boys begged carpet rags from their mothers, rolled them into balls, and after soaking them in oil, lighted them and tossed them into the air as crude skyrockets. Hog bladders, saved from butchering time, were blown up like balloons, dried, and tied to sticks. When held near a stove, fireplace, or bonfire, they exploded with a loud bang. Anvils were commonplace, and "shooting the anvil" was a popular holiday noisemaker. The anvils could be mounted, one on top of the other, with a layer of powder between. When the powder was ignited with a fuse, a deafening roar followed. If only one anvil was available, powder was packed into its hollow and the anvil was set upright on a stump. After the powder was lighted, the anvil flew up in the air with a roar like a cannon. Lacking all else, simply firing rifles or pistols made a satisfying uproar. "Shooting it up" was apparently considered suitable both for celebrating the birth of Jesus and for welcoming in the New Year. An early pioneer woman who lived near Medina remembered: "The New Year's dance would last all night. We always danced the old year out and the new year in. And though we didn't have any fireworks, the boys would watch for the midnight hour and would shoot off pistols outside just at 12."[1]

Drinking and noisemaking were natural companions, and literally staggering amounts of alcohol were drunk to celebrate the season. White lightnin' (whiskey made from corn) and homemade wine and beer were plentiful, but those with cash to spend could buy more refined fuel. As early as 1836 the citizens of Brazoria could purchase wine, brandy, gin, and whiskey from a local merchant. And in 1837, McKinney and Williams in Quintana offered brandy, champagne, cognac, and Holland gin to holiday shoppers. In a letter to his friend James H. Starr, Charles Taylor described the Christmas Eve celebrations at Nacogdoches in 1839: "It is now 9 o'clock, P.M., and tomorrow's Christmas. The way the votaries of that jolly God Bacchus are 'humpin' it is curious. Fiddles groan under a heavy weight of oppression, and heel-taps suffer to the tune of 'We Won't Go Home 'Till Morning,' and now and then the discharge of firearms at a distance, remind me that merriment now despotic rules to the utter discomforture of dull care. . . ."[2]

Sometimes the rough merrymaking bordered on vandalism. Frederick L. Olmsted, a landscape artist and journalist, witnessed such an occasion on Christmas Eve of 1856 in San Augustine when his landlady called him to the window to see the local custom of "The Christmas Serenade": "A band of pleasant spirits started from the square, blowing tin horns, and beating tin pans, and visited in succession every house in the village, kicking in doors, and pulling down fences, until every male member of the family had appeared, with appropriate instruments, and joined the merry party. Then they marched to the square, and ended the ceremony with a centupled tin row."[3]

With guns on their hips and whiskey on their lips, it was inevitable that shoot-outs would occur among the rowdier settlers, and the early Texas newspapers often mentioned such affairs during the Christmas season. The unreliability of early manufactured fireworks and a dare-devil attitude in handling them sometimes led to serious maiming and even some fatalities. Turkey shoots and wild game hunts were more profitable ways to use explosives, as they provided valuable food for holiday meals.

Surveying parties and groups of Texas Rangers often found themselves in remote areas at the holiday season, but with a little luck in their hunting and a little ingenuity on the part of their cooks, they created some memorable feasts. Capt. Jack Elgin, leader of a surveying party for the Houston & Texas Central Railroad, spent Christmas season of 1872 camped with his men near Double Mountain in Stonewall County. On Christmas Eve the surveyors amused themselves hunting, and the Mexican cooks spent the night around a big fire cooking the meat. Sticking the iron ramrods of old muzzle-loading muskets into the ground to hold the spits, they cooked big roasts of the meat over a roaring mesquite fire. At midnight the Mexicans welcomed Christmas Day by firing their guns, which startled the members of the surveying party awake and made them rush out into the snow barefooted, guns in hand and looking for Indians. The cooks were forgiven the next day when they set out a Christmas banquet. Elgin reported:

> I think we had fourteen varieties of meat. We could have had sixteen, as one of our hunters offered to furnish us with a mess of rattlesnakes and polecats, which he assured us were a most excellent delicacy, but our cook drew the line at these. The variety in which the meat was cooked was almost as great as the variety of the meat. We had buffalo, antelope, deer, bear, rabbit, prairie-dog, possum, and possibly other animals that I do not recall; turkey, goose, brant, ducks, prairie-chicken,

curlew, quail, and other birds. The most expensive meat which we had upon the table was bacon, which we had to haul five hundred miles. Of course I had a small supply of bacon to use in a contingency and we took a little to fill up the menu.

Two of the men had killed a young bear on Christmas Eve. The bear had climbed a tree, which they discovered was a bee tree, so they had honey for their dinner also. Elgin had brought along a supply of Borden Condensed Milk, which at that time was a kind of paste. When the can was opened and warm water added, it made good milk. In his medicine chest Elgin had vials of vanilla extract. He gave some of these to his cook to add to the milk. The mixture was set out in the snow for the night, and the next day the group had a large pan of tasty ice cream. "No prince, potentate or magnate ever sat down to such a feast," Elgin declared, no doubt correctly.[4]

In 1875 a group of Rangers, camped in a bend of the San Saba River about three miles east of Menardville, also made a festive holiday by using the bounty of the land. The men had recently been issued Winchester rifles to replace their old Sharps carbines. One of the group, Jim Gillett, recalled:

> The boys were all anxious to try their new guns, and as Christmas approached we decided to have a real Yule-tide dinner. Ed Seiker and myself visited a big turkey-roost on the head of Elm Creek and killed seven big wild turkeys, and on our return Seiker bagged a fine buck deer. J. W. Bell hunted on the San Saba and brought in six or eight wild geese and about a dozen mallard ducks. Donley, the baker, made the pies, while Mrs. Roberts furnished the fruit-cake. Some of the boys made eggnog, and altogether we had the finest Christmas dinner that ever graced the boards of a ranger camp. The village of Menardville was not far away, and most of the rangers visited it during Christmas week for the dancing.[5]

In frontier towns community dances called balls, germans, or hops were popular ways to celebrate.[6] Musical instruments were scarce, but every town had its fiddler, who was frequently the square dance caller as well; many were black men from the community. The dancers moved forward and back, swung their partners, and marched in circles to the caller's commands. When fiddles were not available, the pioneers improvised with mouth organs or simply banged on anything handy—including the wall.

Etiquette required that everyone in the small settlements be invited to dances, even those given in private homes. The rule was "everyone invited and none slighted." A widow who moved to White Mound with her grown children learned this rule the hard way. She gave a Christmas dance and invited only those she and her children wished to ask. Some of the boys who had not been asked were outraged. The next morning the family found all their roosters and hens plucked of their feathers and tied to the picket fence, on which was a large pasteboard sign reading "here is your damn picked crowd."[7]

Subscription balls provided recreation for those who could afford to pay a small fee to participate. The Houston *Telegraph and Texas Register* of December 26, 1838, carried the following invitation: "We have been requested to mention that a Ball will be given in this city on New Years day at the Houston house. The subscription list is now open for those who may wish to participate in the recreation." In San Augustine the eight managers of the ball sent out invitations on pink paper to a cotillion party on Christmas Eve of 1839 at the City Hotel. And in 1840, Adolphus Sterne complained that although the Christmas Eve ball at Nacogdoches went off "tolerable well," it was nothing like the "Old Balls we had in 1833, 4 & 5." He commented that the New Year's Eve ball was *"quite a Business transaction,"* although the ladies "looked as lovely as ever."[8]

"A Ball is soon arranged in these parts, William Bollaert said, "let the room be large or small, it takes place, some friend playing the violin."[9] Everyone from small children to grandparents danced the night away to such tunes as "Pop Goes the Weasel," "Money Musk," and "The Campbells Are Coming." One participant described their dances as the "mazy cotillion, frolicksome reel, dreamy waltz, and fast-moving polka and schottische."[10] Courthouses, with their large rooms, were often used for community holiday dances. Many of the young women rode to the dances sidesaddle on horseback, with long, black riding skirts protecting their party dresses. Under their long skirts, they wore high-top buttoned black shoes and black stockings.

Cowboys living on remote old buffalo ranges in the 1870s liked to celebrate Christmas with lively boot-stomping dances. When Larry Chittenden, reporter for the *New York Times,* arrived in Anson on Christmas Eve of 1885 (or 1887), the proprietor of the Morning Star Hotel invited him to attend a ball being held in the hotel. Chittenden, who later took over the management of a ranch near Anson, was a fascinated spectator at the "lively gaited sworray." Although he took some poetic license in describing the dancers, actually combining balls from several years, Chittenden accurately portrayed the participants and the noisy good time cherished by cowpunchers and their ladies at these free-for-all dances in the poem "The Cowboys' Christmas Ball." In the opening verse he capture the vastness and loneliness of the setting:

> Where the northers come a-whistlin' from beyond the neutral strip
> ·
> Where the coyotes come a-howlin' 'round the Ranches after dark,
> ·
> And the monstrous Stars are winkin' O'er Wilderness profound
> ·
> Where the Antelope is grazin' and the lonely plovers call—
> It was there that I attended "The Cowboys' Christmas Ball."

In the second stanza he characterizes the tiny town of Anson and some local VIPs, including the sheriff and the newspaper editor. The caller is "Windy Bill," who has a voice "like a bugle upon the mountain height." Chittenden's descriptions bring the atmosphere of the ball vividly to life, and it ends:

> The dust riz fast and furious, we all just galloped 'round,
> Till the scenery got so giddy, that Z Bar Dick was downed.
> We buckled to our partners, an' told 'em to hold on,
> Then shook our hoofs like lightning, until the early dawn.[11]

In 1934, the year of Chittenden's death, the Cowboys' Christmas Ball was revived at Anson as an annual presentation, where the old-time dances were reenacted. In 1936, Anson's "Cowboys' Christmas Ball" was featured at the Centennial celebrations in Dallas. And in 1937, it was presented at Chicago's Century of Progress. In 1938, forty dancers presented the ball at the National Folk Festival in Washington and it was broadcast coast to coast on radio.

Each year in Pioneer Hall at Anson's municipal park, dancers wear period costumes and do the old square dances, the Virginia Reel, schottisches, heel-and-toe polkas, put-your-little-foot, as well as country and western dances. On the three or four nights sometime close to Christmas when the ball is held, spectators are welcome to sit in the balcony. The Cowboys' Christmas Ball has come to be known nationally and internationally as a symbol of Texas' Christmas celebrations. Ironically, Anson has a long-standing city ordinance prohibiting dancing–except at Christmastime.

Dancing was prohibited in many frontier towns, and Snap parties became a popular substitute. These parties might be held at various homes every night during the Christmas holidays. The name comes from the original way of choosing a partner, which was to snap one's fingers at the desired person. Couples in the game hold hands, and there is much running and chasing of members of the opposite sex. Car Snap or Swap-Out became popular in the 1930s. It involves the couples' scrambling in and out of cars. Although some adults frowned upon this version of Snap, it has persisted in some non-dancing communities.

Play parties were another way to circumvent the prohibition against dancing. Partners promenaded and skipped, held hands and sang as they moved through their "plays" or "games," carefully avoiding the word "dance." William Owens says the play parties were "a joining of square dancing and children's games" such as "London Bridge is Falling Down," "Drop the Handkerchief," "We're Marching Round the Levee," and "Skip to My Lou."[12] Other favorites of the non-dancing youth were musical chairs, fruit basket turned over, and blindman's buff.

And in addition to all these creative options, corn poppings and candy-pulling parties were also very popular at holiday time. In 1843, William Bollaert, an English traveler in Texas, attended a candy pulling in Huntsville that reminded him of the "Christmas gambols" in his English home. "Some 50 or 60 lads and lasses congregated to assist at this sport. A quantity of molasses is boiled down until it becomes thick; it is then poured out into dishes and plates, each one taking a portion in their hands and commence 'pulling,' or elongating it until it gets cold, when it takes on a yellow appearance and hardens, but the great fun and sport is to approach slyly those persons whose candy appears to be well pulled and snatch it from them, this produces great hilarity."[13]

The custom of having church or community trees and programs evolved with the growing popularity of decorated Christmas trees. In the larger towns the annual programs were apt to be held by individual churches for their own congregations. In frontier communities, they were a group effort. Claudia Davis, who lived in Leakey on the Frio River from 1875 to 1887, remembered working all day with other girls, decorating the large tree at the church: "We all would pop popcorn the day before and string it, so it would be ready to hang on the tree. . . . We didn't have electricity so we had to light the tree and church with candles. When we got the yards and yards of popcorn strings on the tree and the colored paper decorations, and all the presents hung on the branches, it was a pretty sight. We would have apples and oranges hanging on it too, and since we didn't have pretty Christmas paper to wrap our packages in, we would hang the presents on the tree in their boxes if we couldn't get white paper to wrap them in."[14]

The gifts for the children were oranges, apples, nuts, and small toys. The scene was the same for many years in hundreds of little log and rock churches around the state. Kerosene lamps and small, white, homemade candles provided a warm glow for the people who came from remote areas in wagons or on horseback bringing along all the family, no matter how wet or chilly the weather. The fellowship and warmth of these annual Christmas gatherings made them events never to be forgotten in the isolated and hard-bitten lives of the pioneers. In recent years churches, schools, and civic groups in Texas have been increasingly active in sponsoring Christmas programs for children and families.

On Texas plantations, the week between Christmas and New Year's was the traditional holiday highlight of the year, and the Christmas dinner was sumptuous. It might include raw oysters, bear meat, stuffed wild turkey, wild ducks, venison, beef and pork roasts, turnips, greens, sweet potatoes, creamed white potatoes, rice, varieties of home-preserved vegetables and fruits, biscuits and other breads. The meal ended with plum puddings and many kinds of pies and cakes. Eggnog and syllabub were favored drinks, but many imported fine brandies, whiskeys, and wines were also served.

During the holiday week there were religious services, taffy pulls, parties, dances, and entertainment provided by slaves. In the evening there were fireworks. Dried hog bladder balloons were used, as well as gunpowder in various forms. Often weddings were combined with the Christmas celebrations in towns and on plantations. Smaller planters, too, entertained as much as they could afford. John Frazier, the seven-year-old son of a cotton planter in Bosque county, spent a memorable 1868 holiday. His father introduced cotton into the county, selling his first crop that year for thirty-six cents a pound, gold. On the strength of this bounty, there were brass-toed, red-topped boots for the boys of the family and the first wool hats they had even seen. The highlight of the day was a party given by the Fraziers. They invited neighbors from twenty miles around to see the "first fireworks display west of Waco." The grown-ups were almost as excited as the children as they watched firecrackers, Roman candles, and skyrockets fill the night with sound and color.

Like plantations, ranches in Texas were far apart, and getting together for the holidays presented problems. Cattlemen and cowboys liked to celebrate the season with dances, but female partners were hard to come by, and there are tales of ranchers traveling a hundred or two hundred miles round-trip to fetch a female dancing partner. And there were no disparaging remarks when a cowboy became a designated female partner by tying a handkerchief around his arm or leg.

The difficulty of getting together made the holidays all the more appreciated. Ralph Semmes Jackson, who came from a large family, remembered the celebrations on an East Texas ranch in Chambers County: "The Clan would start arriving a week before Christmas and would linger on for at least a week after. Some came by boat from Galveston and some by rail to White's Ranch, where they were met by a member of the family and transported by buggy or wagon eighteen miles across the prairie to the ranch house. Some Christmases as many as twenty-five guests would gather for the Christmas holidays."[15] Old Fanny, the family cook, fed two or three shifts of diners three big meals each day. Behind the locked pantry door were barrels of provisions, including all kinds of nuts and crates of apples and oranges, which were shipped in through Galveston. Everything down to the whipped cream for pancakes was homemade.

At the beginning of Christmas week a huge oak backlog was wrestled into the fireplace, where it burned for a week. The children eagerly anticipated the hunting expedition to find the right Christmas tree, usually a tall pine, and holly for decorating. After the tree was placed in the parlor, the doors were tightly closed. The adults enjoyed decorating and redecorating it, and the children relished the delicious suspense until eight P.M. on Christmas Eve, when the parlor doors were thrown open. Jackson remembered:

> There it stood in a blaze of flickering candlelight, stretching from floor to ceiling and from wall to wall. Surely there were a thousand Christmas candles, the glowing flame of each reflected from the strings of gold and silver tinsel and from countless glistening varicolored balls. Strings of snow-white popcorn traced a delicate pattern of graceful loops and swirls against the deep green of the pine needles. A swinging apple or orange would be reflected in an occasional dull red or orange glow. Each limb was heavy laden with presents, as all, except the most bulky were tied to the branches of the tree. High up near the top would be the dolls for the little girls. Below the dolls were the presents for the boys and adults.[16]

Christmas dinner on the Jackson Ranch was lavish. There were ducks, ham, turkey with cornbread stuffing and gravy, hot biscuits, sweet potatoes with marshmallows, corn with cream and butter, butter beans, string beans, peas, and Waldorf salad; for dessert, mincemeat, pumpkin, and custard pies, coconut layer cake, fruitcake, chocolate layer cake, seven-layer jelly cake, and a traditional Scottish cake with a hard icing.

On the Goodnight (JA) Ranch, Colonel Goodnight entertained the whole Panhandle with a big holiday party. Long tables set up in the form of a cross held loads of beef, turkey, antelope, cakes, pies, and many other dishes. A spruce or other evergreen from Palo Duro Canyon stood where the long tables met. The tree was decorated with bunches of frosted raisins and strings of popcorn and cranberries. Each of the guests received a gift. The ranchers and their cowboys enjoyed dancing until daybreak. Since there were never enough women at the dances, the men had to take turns with the women who were there.

Also in the Panhandle, Henry and Lizzie Campbell dispensed generous hospitality at the "White House" on the Matador Ranch, inviting cowboys, neighbors (within a radius of over twenty miles), travelers, and anyone "who needed a home to observe Christmas." The first annual Christmas party at the ranch was saved only by Mrs. Campbell's ingenuity when the Christmas "makings" ordered from Fort Worth failed to arrive until March 1, because of the slowness of the ox team. She used popcorn and odd scraps of colored material to trim a native cedar, and for Christmas dinner she prepared "wild turkeys, larded liberally with strips of bacon which came from wild hogs on the range, cornbread dressing, boiled hams, venison steaks, a huge pot of antelope stew with dumplings [which the cowboys called sinkers], wild rice, corn pudding, apple pies from dried apples, and a washtub full of doughnuts. Wild plum jelly substituted for cranberry sauce."[17] The Christmas ball at the Matador became a tradition similar to the one at Anson, and trimming the Christmas tree prior to the dance was part of the fun.

Guests who visited the main house on the King Ranch in South Texas were reminded of large English manor houses. Once a year at the annual Christmas party for the workers (kineños), Henrietta King relaxed her strict rules against dancing. All the ranch hands and their families gathered for the party, and Mrs. King (La Patrona) distributed traditional gifts of shirts and petticoats for the adults and tarlatan stockings filled with fruit and candy for the children.

J. Frank Dobie recalled Christmas on his family ranch twenty-seven miles from Beeville. Three or four times a year a wagon went into town to haul supplies, with the biggest haul just before Christmas. Ambrosia, made with oranges and fresh coconut, was a special holiday treat. Dobie remembered stockings stuffed with oranges, apples, and raisins—all seasonal treats. He also remembered the noises of the holiday made with firecrackers and dried hog-bladder balloons. The Dobie children always got books for Christmas. *Ivanhoe* turned the boys into knights, and *Swiss Family Robinson* made them cave dwellers. Each Christmas there was a large wooden bucket of mixed candy for the six Dobie children to share with visiting cousins and with the children of several Mexican families living on the ranch.

The XIT Ranch in northern Texas had the reputation of holding the best dances in the country while serving nothing stronger than coffee. In 1909 the managers of the XIT planned a Christmas party at Buffalo Springs, headquarters of the most northern of the seven divisions of the vast ranch. Everybody in the town of Channing plus everyone in the surrounding country was invited. A fiddle and a piano furnished the music. The women wore white Gibson shirtwaists with full skirts, some fifteen feet around at the bottom, and the cowboys wore suits ordered from Kansas City and Chicago. Most amazing to all of the guests, who were used to a diet of cornbread, beans, and salt pork, was the feast spread on a fifteen-foot-long table: "In the center was a big roast pig with an apple in his mouth. He was flanked by roast beef, roast turkey, chickens and wild ducks. There were pies and cakes and piles of apples and oranges. The children, who had never seen an orange, were in ecstasy."[18]

Christmas holidays were as much of an oasis for Texas soldiers as they were for Texas cowboys. Since the purpose of the far-flung string of forts was to protect settlers against Indians, the forts were built in lonely areas ahead of western settlement. Homesickness increased in the garrisons as Christmas approached; thoughts turned to home, and soldiers sometimes deserted. One solution was to keep the men busy preparing for dances and parties, decorating their barracks, and planning holiday feasts. Officers, noncommissioned officers, and individual troops held numerous entertainments, large and small, during a long holiday period.

Fort Davis usually held a grand ball on Christmas Eve in one of the enlisted men's barracks. Dancing began at nine P.M., and officers and their wives attended, along with invited guests from nearby communities. After a midnight supper, dancing continued for several hours until the band played "Home, Sweet Home" to signal that the party was over. In 1883, Troop B of the Tenth Cavalry hosted the ball. The men set up two Christmas trees laden with "every variety of fruit" and sponsored a waltz contest with a large chocolate cake as the prize.

Children at Fort Davis were given special parties with refreshments and presents, the post commander himself acting as Santa Claus. A second Santa, played by an enlisted man, drove around the garrison in a mule-drawn wagon distributing candy to the children at their quarters. Christmas dinner was the most splendid meal of the year and a welcome change from the soldiers' usual monotonous fare. Dances and open houses welcomed in the New Year.

Because there were so few children at the forts, officers and enlisted men alike doted on them. Fort Concho was called a "children's zoo" because of the many pets that had been given to the children. In 1873 Col. Wesley Merritt and his wife, who had no children of their own, gave a party for the children of the garrison. Their home, Quarters No. 1, was gaily decorated with a large tree holding gifts that Colonel

Merritt, dressed as Santa, handed out to the children. When Benjamin Henry Grierson replaced Colonel Merritt in Quarters No. 1, his family continued the custom of giving big Christmas parties for all the children on the post.

In 1875 the Griersons gave an elaborate party using game that the colonel had brought back from a hunting expedition. In addition to the antelope, venison, goose, and eight wild turkeys, the cook prepared a ham, three fruitcakes, three marble cakes, two jelly cakes, and two white cakes. The Griersons also entertained with a dance and had an open house on New Year's Day.

The pecking order at the forts was observed in all areas of life, even in the holiday dances. At Fort Concho these were held in the mess tent or in a barracks. The officers and their dates danced with each other at one end of the building, while the enlisted men danced with laundresses, servants, women from the community, or each other. The band sat in the middle of the building and played for both groups.

Although there were typically two hundred to three hundred enlisted men at Fort Concho, the chaplain saw few of them (or of the officers) at regular Sunday worship. He usually had to be content to preach to about thirty officers' wives and children. But at Christmastime the place of worship was decorated with evergreens and mistletoe, and the chaplain happily noted in his report that "nearly the whole garrison turned out."[19]

In recent years Fort Concho has come to life annually with a Christmas celebration called Christmas at Old Fort Concho. This celebration features six of the well-preserved two-story houses on Officers' Row, which are decorated in historical themes: a Mexican house, a German house, a Czech house, a Victorian house, an early Texas house, and a house representing a typical officer's quarters. Other buildings are occupied by a sutler's store, a barracks decorated to show how the soldiers spent Christmas, and an old-time saloon (which would have been found not on the post, but across the river in the then-corrupt village of San Angelo). Ethnic foods are sold and there are craft demonstrations. The Fort Concho Memorial Infantry, Cavalry, and Buffalo Soldier units perform marching and rifle drills. "A Fort Concho Christmas Carol" depicting the history of the fort is performed each evening. Like the Dickens evening at Galveston, the event is growing each year and attracting thousands of people interested in what holiday celebrations were like in nineteenth-century Texas.

Settlers brought to Texas the Americanized Santa Claus, who developed from the European Saint Nicholas. Born in Lycia, now a part of Turkey, in the A.D. 300s, Nicholas became a bishop. Many legends grew up about him, both during his life and after his death. One is that he saved three impoverished girls from prostitution by giving them bags of gold to use as dowries. Another is that he could bring ships safely through wild storms. He was famous for giving generously to the needy, especially to children. After his death, he became the favorite saint of children in Belgium, the Netherlands, Germany, and other northern and central European countries. His feast day, December 6, became a day for celebrations and for gift giving.

Dutch settlers brought the custom of celebrating Saint Nicholas Day to New Amsterdam (New York City). American children quickly adopted the saint, but they had difficulty pronouncing the Dutch name *Sant Nikolaas* and called him Santy, or Santa, Claus. In the New World his appearance also underwent a change from the tall, thin, serious European bishop to the fat, jolly Santa of modern times. Washington Irving pictured him as a happy, rotund fellow wearing wide Dutchman's breeches and smoking a long clay pipe. Clement Moore's poem "'Twas the Night before Christmas" (1823) added twinkling eyes, a nose like a cherry, and a white beard and gave him a sleigh with eight reindeer to carry him on his rounds.[20] The finishing touches to the Santa Claus imported to Texas were added by Thomas Nast, a newspaper cartoonist of the Civil War era, and Haddon Sundblom, an illustrator who did advertisements for the Coca-Cola company in the 1930s.

Many of our traditional Christmas carols were brought to Texas by American settlers. "We Three Kings of Orient Are," which has achieved international popularity, is among the enduring favorites. A famous American minister, Phillips Brooks, was inspired to write "O Little Town of Bethlehem" after a visit to Christ's birthplace. Henry Wadsworth Longfellow wrote the words to "I Heard the Bells on Christmas Day" to express his feelings after his son was seriously wounded in the Civil War. He did not intend it as a carol, yet this sad but hopeful song has become a message of comfort to those with troubled spirits at Christ-

mastime. The founder and editor of *Scribner's Magazine* wrote the words to "There's a Song in the Air," which was set to music by a college professor. And the text of "It Came upon the Midnight Clear" was written by Edmund Sears, a Harvard-trained Unitarian clergyman.

In the twentieth century, American composers have continued to write Christmas songs that are perennial favorites in Texas as well as the rest of the nation. These include "Jingle Bells," "Up on the Housetop," "Frosty the Snowman," "White Christmas," "Rudolph the Red-nosed Reindeer," and "Santa Claus Is Coming to Town."

O. Henry, a writer to whom Texas lays some claim, has been called the American Dickens, and like Dickens he has made enduring contributions to Christmas literature. "The Gift of the Magi," "The Cop and the Anthem," and "Whistling Dick's Christmas Stocking" are stories that have passed the test of time.

Immigrants from the southern states carried into Texas the tradition of eating black-eyed peas on New Year's Day for good luck. The rules regarding the condition of the peas (dried, fresh, frozen) are held important by many Texans, who get into impassioned discussions about this. Tomatoes, onions, and corn bread traditionally accompany the black-eyed peas. Southerners also brought to Texas treasured recipes for their fabulous pies. Since buttermilk and pecans were usually readily available, these two pies were often served at holiday meals.[21]

Buttermilk Pie

1 unbaked 9-inch pie shell	3 eggs, beaten
¼ cup flour	½ cup buttermilk
1¾ cups sugar	1 t. vanilla
½ t. salt	1 t. lemon extract
½ cup butter, melted	sprinkling of nutmeg (optional)

Combine flour, sugar, and salt in a bowl. Add melted butter and beaten eggs, and beat slightly with rotary beater. Stir in buttermilk, beating with a spoon and blending in flavoring. Pour into unbaked pastry shell. Sprinkle with nutmeg. Bake at 350° for 45–50 minutes. Let cool before cutting.

Southern Pecan Pie

1 unbaked 9-inch pie shell	2 T. milk
1 cup light brown sugar, firmly packed	1 t. vanilla
½ cup white sugar	½ cup butter, melted (do not substitute)
1 T. flour	1 cup pecans, chopped
2 eggs	

Mix brown sugar, white sugar, and flour. Add eggs, milk, vanilla, and melted butter; beat well. Fold in pecans. Pour into unbaked pastry shell. Bake in 375° oven 40–50 minutes. Serve slightly warm. Top servings with whipped cream or ice cream if desired.

Early Anglo-American Texans often led hardscrabble lives, and many of their holiday celebrations were impromptu and spontaneous. Evidence of their creativity in making Christmas gifts can be seen in museums where rag and cornshuck dolls, whittled toys, string balls, and pieces of embroidery and crochet that once hung on pioneer Christmas trees are displayed. These Anglo-American settlers had to know how to make do with whatever was available, and they contributed traditions and customs to Texas that have become tightly woven into our pattern of celebrating Christmas.

Keeping the Faith:

THE AFRICAN-AMERICAN HERITAGE

Christmas Gift! Estevan, sometimes called Stephen the Moor, was the first known black man in Texas. A companion of Cabeza de Vaca, he had a reputation as a wonder-healer and also as a guide. In 1539, he was killed by Indians in southwest Texas. Blacks also accompanied Coronado on his expeditions, and some came with Alarcón, the founder of San Antonio, and remained in that settlement. In early Spanish settlements in Texas, a few blacks, both free and slave, lived. The majority of African-Americans in Texas in the nineteenth century, however, were brought in as slaves by white agriculturists. Some had also been smuggled in by slave traders before the nineteenth century with the cooperation of the pirate Jean Lafitte.

Life for slaves on Texas farms and plantations was hard and monotonous, and the Christmas season was eagerly looked toward. Time was marked as being "so far to Christmas." Since the cotton crop had been picked and shipped by then, many planters gave their slaves the week as a holiday except for necessary chores, such as feeding livestock, milking, and gathering eggs. These and the household chores were shared among the house servants, so each got some time off. The big house was decorated from top to bottom with greenery and candles, and slaves cut and hauled an enormous tree into the best parlor. They took particular care in choosing the large Yule log to place at the back of the parlor fireplace, as the tradition on many plantations was that the holidays would last as long as the Yule log burned.

The customary greeting in December was "Christmas Gift!" rather than "Merry Christmas!" And although gift giving among adults was not common early in the century, most planters gave their servants presents. Often the gifts were clothing or shoes to supplement their scanty wardrobes. They also gave gifts to slave children; these might include pennies, a sack of candy, or a popcorn ball. One unusually generous planter gave each of his slave families a present of twenty-five dollars—*real* money in the mid-nineteenth century. Among the whites there was a constant round of visiting at Christmastime, and the visitors often tossed small trinkets or pieces of money to the servants who waited on them.

The diet of slaves improved considerably during the holidays. Christmas memories of two former slaves are recorded in the *Texas Slave Narratives*. Andrew Moody, who lived in Orange County, told his interviewer: "Folks had good times Christmas. Dancin' and big dinner. They given 'em two or three day holiday then. They give Christmas gif', maybe a pair stockin's or sugar candy. The white folks kill turkey and set table for the slaves with everything like they have, bread and biscuit and cake and po'k and baked turkey and chicken and sich."[1] And John Price, who lived near Liberty, recalled: "Us ol' boss man say Crissmus day was his day to treat. He tell us 'bout Santy Claus. Us taken us sox up to de boss' house and hang dem dat away 'roun de big fireplace, and den in de mawnin' us find candy and cake and fruit and hab a big time. New Year' Day was ol' mistus time. She fix a big dinner for eb'rybody on dat day and nobody hafter wuk."[2] Other former slaves recalled having white bread instead of corn bread as a special holiday treat, and others had memories of 'possum and sweet potatoes swimming in molasses.

In 1856, Lucadia Pease, wife of Gov. E. M. Pease, wrote to her family back East: "Our servants gave a Christmas party and had a handsome supper—a turkey, pair of ducks and chicken, roast beef, and two large loaves of cake, with coffee, biscuits . . . made the table look quite inviting."[3]

William Bollaert, an English visitor to Texas in 1843, witnessed a New Year's ball in Huntsville held for the blacks of the area in an unfinished store. He observed the slaves' holiday week between Christmas and New Year's. "Bedecked out in their best," they visited each other and spent the evenings singing and dancing. At the New Year's dance they were introduced by the names of their masters and mistresses. The dancing was vigorous with "each limb in movement" and the laughter "truly joyous and hearty." At midnight they had a supper. Then they danced until daylight, when they had to return to their homes.[4]

Spirited dancing freed the slaves' spirits for a few hours from the oppression of their bondage. Juba, a complex dance involving rhythmic clapping and body movements, is probably of West African origin, with the patting technique handed down from generation to generation. Blacks' square dances were free and wild, with the caller making up the words as he went along. Dances with vigorous motions such as round dances, pigeon wings, buck-and-wings, and freestyle gallops released the dancers' minds and bodies.

Singing was another release. Slaves often worked to the rhythm of spirituals. The rhythmic tunes and simple, often moving lyrics of seasonal spirituals deepened the celebration of Christmas. Like some European folk carols, spirituals portray the Holy Family empathetically—in terms of the singers themselves. An example of this empathy is "O Po' Little Jesus":

> O, poor Little Jesus
> This world gonna break Your heart.
> There'll be no place to lay Your head, my Lord,
> O, poor Little Jesus."[5]

And the chanted refrain ("Wasn't that a pity? Wasn't that a shame?") seems to come from the singers' understanding, increasing the sympathetic feeling of the song.

"Behold That Star" was written by the son of a former slave who wanted to write a jubilee song about Christmas. The famous, but anonymous, spiritual "Go Tell It on the Mountain" expresses the joy and the mystery of Christmas:

> When I was a seeker, I sought both night and day;
> I asked the Lord to help me, And he showed me the way.
>
> He made me a watchman, Upon the city wall;
> And if I am a Christian, I am the least of all.
>
> Go tell it on the mountain, Over the hills and everywhere;
> Go tell it on the mountain, That Jesus Christ is born.[6]

Almost nothing is known about the composition of other favorite spirituals such as "Rise Up, Shepherd, and Follow," and "Mary Had a Baby" with its refrain "O Lord, O My Lord, O Lord, the people keep a-coming and the train done gone."[7]

Also lost in a long process of oral tradition is the authorship of the popular counting carol "Children Go Where I Send Thee," in which the verses accumulate in reverse order:

I'm going to send thee one by one [two by two, three by three . . .]
1. One for the little bitty Baby,
2. Two for Paul and Silas,
3. Three for the Hebrew children,
4. Four for the four that stood at the door.
5. Five for the gospel preachers.
6. Six for the six that never got fixed.
7. Sev'n for the sev'n that never went to Heav'n.
8. Eight for the eight that stood at the gate.
9. Nine for the nine that dressed so fine.
10. Ten for the Ten Commandments.
Born – Born – Born in Bethlehem.[8]

Much of what is referred to as "good ol' southern cooking" was created by black women who knew how to turn everyday foods such as sweet potatoes and corn meal into delicious dishes for holiday eating. Many blacks still make these dishes an important part of their Christmastime dinner table.[9]

Sweet Potato Pone
Geraldine Terrell

6 medium sweet potatoes, peeled	½ t. cloves
2 cups brown sugar	1 cup molasses
1 stick butter or margarine	6 eggs, beaten
½ t. cinnamon	2 T. flour
½ t. nutmeg	1 cup milk
½ t. allspice	

Grate potatoes. Mix all ingredients well, and cook in greased 9×9-inch deep baking dish at 350° until set and slightly brown on top. Makes 6–8 servings.

Texans of African-American descent face extraordinary difficulty in trying to trace their heritage since many of their ancestors lost track of even their family names. When slaves gained their freedom, they often

Corn Bread
Imogene White

2 cups buttermilk   2 t. sugar
2 eggs   1 t. salt
1 t. baking soda   drop of vanilla
2 cups yellow corn meal   1 t. melted butter

Combine buttermilk, eggs, and soda, and beat well. Mix together corn meal, sugar, and salt. Add buttermilk mixture, and mix well. Add vanilla. Pour into 9×9×2-inch baking pan coated with 1 t. melted butter. Bake at 450° about 20 minutes. Makes 8–10 servings.

took the names of their former owners. After the Civil War many blacks wanted to blot out the past and think only of making a better future. Recently, however, there has been a concerted effort to discover roots and use the past to make a better present.

An Ethiopian holiday called Kwanza (also spelled Kwanzaa)–first fruits or harvest–has been imported into the United States and into Texas. A traditional celebration, Kwanza runs from December 26 through January 1. A candle is lit on each of the seven days to symbolize seven principles that can help blacks change their lives for the better. These *nguzo saba* (seven principles of blackness) are:

1. Unity–in the family, community, nation, and race
2. Self-determination–defining oneself instead of being defined by others
3. Collective Work and Responsibility–solving problems together
4. Cooperative Economics–building and maintaining businesses together
5. Purposes–building and developing the community in order to restore black people to their traditional greatness
6. Creativity–making the community more beautiful and more beneficial
7. Faith–"To believe with all our heart in our parents, our teachers, our people and the righteousness and victory of our struggle."[10]

To purify their bodies, minds, and spirits, blacks celebrating Kwanza fast from sunrise to sunset. Homes are decorated with symbolic colors: red for the blood of their ancestors; black for their race; and green for land and youth, their future and their reason to struggle and survive.

Other symbols are also used to help reinforce their principles. A straw mat (*Mkeka*) is put on a low table or on the floor. It represents the foundation on which all else rests, and all the items for Kwanza are placed on it. *Muhindi* is an ear of corn. As many *Muhindi* are used as there are children in the family. The kernels represent the children and the stalk represents the father. Children in the family draw pictures of the sun (representing creation and growth) and the ankh (symbol of life and man).

The week of celebration ends with a potluck feast. At midnight the seventh candle (for faith) is lit, and the group sings and dances. On January 1 children are given educational gifts (books) or gifts made by their parents. A number of black families in San Antonio have celebrated Kwanza since 1966, when it was brought to the United States by sociologist Maulana Karenga. The purpose of Kwanza, says its founder, is "to give thanks and to make a joyful noise in a meaningful and traditional way"–a good objective for any celebration.

FRÖHLICHE
WEIHNACHTEN

wünscht

E. Richter.

O Tannenbaum:

THE GERMAN HERITAGE

Fröhe Weihnachten! German immigrants began coming to Texas in the waning years of Mexican rule and during the days of the Republic. The largest number of Germans, however, were brought in by the Adelsverein, or Association of Noblemen. The Verein tried to protect the German immigrants until they could manage for themselves after their first crops were harvested. In 1844, the Verein sent a quixotic leader, Prince Carl Solms-Braunfels, to Texas to make preparations for more German immigrants and to help the German settlers already in Texas. The prince secured the services of the first known German Protestant minister in Texas, the Rev. Louis C. Ervendberg, who had been in Texas since 1839. In 1844 the Reverend Ervendberg conducted Christmas Eve services in Port Lavaca, using as a Christmas tree a large oak, decorated with candles and presents for the children. Prince Solms furnished the presents and the tree, which was probably the first public Christmas tree in Texas.

Where the early settlers were more scattered, communal celebrating was not always possible. But a German immigrant, Gustav Dresel, found a way to liven up the season in Montgomery County. Spending a quiet Christmas Eve with his landlord, another German, talking about their homeland and reading German poems, Dresel felt homesick. Dresel said, "This prosaic life did not please me. I designed a plan to prepare new enjoyments for these backwoods people." The plan he devised came from an old German tradition of "shooting in Christmas." With a fellow conspirator, Dresel galloped to Montgomery and bought four jugfuls of whiskey, as much as their saddlebags would hold. Then he set about recruiting men with guns and powder. The liquor, though "unspeakably bad," acted like a charm in enlisting aid. "Whenever it is a matter of organizing a frolic, a spree, the Texians are not found wanting," Dresel noted approvingly.

With his cohorts he galloped from farm to farm, firing guns into the air. Children cried, dogs howled, and households were thrown into panic, thinking they were being attacked by Indians or Mexicans. The astonished men of the house were handed the jugs and invited to join the fun. Volunteers were picked up at each stop, and by midnight there were fifteen riders. At the last stop they were asked in for a feast of stag's ham, maize cake, and eggnog made with the last of their bad whiskey. At daybreak the men returned to their scattered homes, well satisfied with their celebration, declaring Dresel "a hell of a Dutchman."[1]

In 1845, Ferdinand von Roemer, a German naturalist, was pleased to celebrate the holidays with "the jolly companionship of the Verein's officers in New Braunfels around a richly decorated and illuminated cedar Christmas tree." As Roemer gazed at the tree, he reminisced, "On the same place where today the symbols of a happy German family life is planted in the midst of a cultured population, scarcely two years ago the camp fires of the wild Comanches were burning."[2]

Seven sisters living in a seven-gabled house in the heart of Texas have been keeping alive the spirit of traditional German Christmases for over half a century. Today, although only three of the Timmermann sisters are living, they continue to celebrate the season joyfully and to share the Timmermann Tannenbaum and their treasured heritage with hundreds of visitors. Their fame has spread far beyond the tiny town of Geronimo, near Seguin. They have appeared on national and local TV shows and have been featured in national magazines, as well as in dozens of local newspapers and magazines. They have also taken their show on the road by displaying their famous tree and miniatures at the Institute of Texan Cultures in San Antonio. Their annual Christmas display, in the 1892 farmhouse built by their father, attracts hundreds of visitors each December. The sisters, dressed in matching costumes, tell again and again the story behind their Christmas celebration.

The seven sisters spent sixty-eight Christmases together from the birth of the youngest, Willie Mae, in 1916 to the death of Estella, 85, in 1984. Like their German father, the sisters still consider it important to select and decorate the perfect huge cedar tree each year, even though they no longer personally cut and drag it out of the woods. Cookies, apples, oranges, tinsel stars, heirloom paper, and gilded ornaments fill its branches, and some of the ornaments on their tree are well over a hundred years old. But the miniature scenes under the tree create the most excitement for the busloads of children who come to the farmhouse each holiday season. Amid ferns and honeycomb rocks stands an elaborate crèche with an overhanging cloud of angels. A skilled plumber worked four days to install an intricate system of pipes to produce a waterfall and the Guadalupe River, where a deer drinks and two boys lie on their stomachs forever peering into a fishing hole. The Timmermann farm kitchen is reproduced down to tiny braided rugs and cedar wreaths.

The most historical miniature under the Timmermann tree is of the orphanage established by the Rev. Louis C. Ervendberg, the Timmermann sisters' great-grandfather. After a shipload of incoming German settlers had been ravaged by sickness in 1846, the Ervendbergs took nineteen orphans to raise with their own five children. The illuminated replica of the orphanage has tiny carved furnishings and figures showing Indians peering through a window at the children, who are celebrating Christmas as a visitor described it during a visit there in 1849.[3]

The visitor was Hermann Seele, a German schoolteacher in New Braunfels. In his diary Seele relates that after he was greeted by the Ervendbergs and the children in neat clothing and wearing new Christmas caps, he was led into the schoolroom that had been converted into a Christmas setting: "To the right stood the Christmas tree, a magnificent young cedar, and underneath I discovered a small garden. Beautiful honey comb rocks were placed to represent distant hills. In the foreground on the green grass stood the miniature shepherds from Bethlehem herding their miniature flocks. In the center on a flat rock stood the manger with the sleeping Christ Child."[4] The children whispered to him that for eight weeks the girls had been sewing suits and knitting stockings for the boys and crocheting gifts for each other. The boys had braided whips for each other. They had combined efforts to make a knitted bedspread for Mrs. Ervendberg. Their gift making was in the German tradition of giving something of oneself by making Christmas gifts by hand.

The food, prepared by the girls, was homemade and simple. Seele especially enjoyed the canned wild plum and grape compote, the clear sparkling wine made of wild mustang grapes, the raisin bread, and the Christmas punch. During the week Seele spent at the orphanage, the evening entertainment included lively games, songs, riddles, and story telling. The orphanage at New Wied, now Gruene, still stands and is occupied by descendants of the Ervendbergs, who still have treasured ornaments from the days when Seele made his visit.

German settlers such as John O. Meusebach, founder of Fredericksburg, trimmed their evergreens, but decorated Christmas trees were still a novelty in most of the United States when Seele visited the New Braunfels orphanage. The origin of the German tree goes back to a popular medieval play about Adam and Eve. The Paradise tree (a fir hung with apples) was the most important prop in the play. Then German families began setting up Paradise trees in their homes on December 24, the religious feast day of Adam and Eve. Wafers symbolizing Communion bread and candles symbolizing Christ as the light of the world were added to it.

Another German innovation that found favor as a decoration was the *lichtstock*, a pyramid of wooden shelves on which many small lighted candles were placed. Called the poor man's Christmas tree, these little trees were made in a circular shape and sometimes included tiny wooden umbrellas on top that revolved from the heat of the candles. In the sixteenth century some German homes had in the same room as the Paradise tree a Christmas *lichtstock*, holding Christmas figurines and evergreen branches with a star at the top. The Paradise trees and Christmas pyramids merged into the modern Christmas tree. Today, however, some intricately carved *lichtstocks* are made by German carvers as table decorations.

In the 1800s some German immigrants brought the first artificial trees to Texas. These were made of turkey feathers that were dyed green, wound onto wire branches, and mounted on wooden bases. They ranged eventually from a two-inch size carried by a Saint Nicholas figure to a ninety-eight-inch size sold in a United States department store in the 1920s. Today the feather trees are rare collector's items.

When Christmas trees were introduced by homesick German settlers in the eastern United States in such cities as Boston and Philadelphia, they were denounced as sacrilegious and pagan by some Protestant groups. The scholarly members of the Texas Verein, however,

brought with them a legend that justified the practice. According to this legend, not only shepherds and wise men went to worship the new-born Christ Child in Bethlehem, but trees also made the journey. The spruce traveled the farthest and was the most scraggly and drab of all the trees—until stars dropped from the sky, clinging to its branches and sprinkling its gray leaves with their silvery dust. The star of Bethlehem came to rest on the topmost twig. When the baby Jesus saw the tree, he laughed with delight at its twinkling beauty. And since then trees have been decorated on Christmas Eve to make the hearts of children glad as a tribute to the Christ Child. This charming legend and the friendly glow of the lighted trees helped decorated trees become a firmly entrenched Texas tradition.

Of necessity, in Texas the German Tannenbaum or fir tree was replaced by the cedar or juniper. Until a few years ago, the tradition of an outing to find and cut just the right tree continued in many German families, and it still remains a happy event among some Hill Country families. Before cheap factory-made ornaments were available around the turn of the century, tree decorations were made from whatever was at hand.[5] Most common among Germans were popcorn chains, paper flowers, paper chains made of stiff colored paper, other more intricate paper ornaments, decorated cookies, candy and nuts wrapped in bright scraps of paper, ribbons, bits of glass and metal, polished fruit, and homemade candles. German descendants who were children at the turn of the century remember the special aroma of apples and oranges hanging on Christmas trees because these fruits were rare treats that appeared only at that time of year. Wise parents did not permit the candy decorations to be eaten until the tree came down, undoubtedly making the children more willing to see the destruction of the magical tree.

The glow and flicker of the wax candles clipped to its branches added to the magic of the tree. These twinkling lights also added an element of danger and excitement, especially in wooden churches where towering cedars of twenty feet or more were common. If the decorators followed the advice of a magazine published in the late 1800s, which suggested using four hundred candles for a twelve-foot tree, the hazard must have been great indeed. And there were instances where Santas got their cotton beards too near the trees and turned into flaming torches. At church celebrations the trustees stood by with wet sponges on long sticks or other snuffing devices to extinguish candles as they burned low, and in both homes and churches the celebrators kept buckets of water or sand handy.

German settlers introduced two other enduring customs involving the use of candles. Their traditional Advent wreath is a variation of the English Advent wreath. Each of the five candles is a different color and has a different meaning. There is a purple candle for prophecy, a green candle for Bethlehem, a blue candle for the shepherds, and a gold candle for the angels. On Christmas Day the fifth, white candle representing the Christ Child is lit.[5] Germans also placed a candle in a window so the Christ Child, who might be wandering in the dark streets, would know he was welcome to enter. Candles may still be seen in many windows at Christmastime in Texas, although the original reason for putting them there may no longer be remembered.

Germans found ways of adapting to their new surroundings to decorate for the holidays. They used cedars as Christmas trees, they decorated homes and churches with cedar branches, and they burned cedar twigs in fireplaces to create a holiday aroma. In Germany mistletoe has long been regarded as having magical properties, so the immigrants in the central Texas area were pleased to find it in large quantities and used it in their decorating as well.

"Kris Kringle" comes from the German word for Christ Child— *Christkindlein*. A few generations ago German children were taught that the Christ Child was the bringer as well as the receiver of gifts on his birth night. Legend has it that Martin Luther tried to establish the idea of the Christ Child as the giver of gifts because he felt that Saint Nicholas was diverting too much attention from the reason for the celebration. But Saint Nicholas, one of the most popular saints of the Christian church, was not to be ousted, for he was especially revered by children.

Like King Arthur, who is based on a real man but grew to be larger than life, Saint Nicholas (A.D. 300s) has evolved from a real man into one who is credited with supernatural abilities. He has become fused with various pagan and secular gift givers. But in the tradition brought to Texas by German immigrants, he is a separate and distinct figure, tall and thin, dressed in his bishop's robes, quite unlike our jolly, fat Santa in his bright red suit. In earlier times his visit to the German children was like a Judgment Day. He checked on their behavior, rewarding the good ones with small gifts of nuts and fruits and leaving the naughty ones warning switches. Parents had only to mention his name to ensure good behavior from December 6, Saint Nicholas Day, to December 25. German celebrations in the early years of the twentieth century emphasized proper, pious behavior by children. In *Coffee in the Gourd* Julia Estill describes a Texas Hill Country Christmas among the Germans.

On the twenty-fourth of December, she relates, at least one Santa Claus came to the homes:

> He enters about the time the candles on the cedar tree are lighted and the home circle is gathered in the "best room." Every child is then asked to pray. This is the little petition the children lisp: "Ich bin klein, mein Herz ist rein; soll niemand drin wohnen als Jesus allein" (I am small; my heart is pure; no one shall abide there save Jesus alone).

> Santa, being satisfied, then leaves an apple or an orange with each child and repairs to the neighboring house,—if the children have all responded with the prayer. But woe to the unruly youngster, usually a sophisticated boy, who refuses to pray! He is soundly rapped with the huge stick Santa carries concealed under his mantle. Sometimes two or three of these Santa Clauses visit the same house in a single evening; and the program is usually repeated each time.[6]

Gilbert Jordan also recalls a traditional St. Nicholas: "Sometime between December 6 and Christmas Eve, *Sankt Nikolaus* came to check up on the little children. We were afraid of this stern European character, but we usually escaped his wrath and switch when our parents vouched for our goodness and we said our prayers before him. Then he gave us some treats and called us good children."[7] In the Jordan family it was the adults and some of the older children who decorated the tree on the afternoon of Christmas Eve, behind locked doors. The little children were told that the *Weihnachtsmann*—Father Christmas—might bring them presents that evening, but they never saw him, although they sometimes thought they heard him moving about. In their imaginations he was a pedestrian, who trudged from house to house, not the driver of a sleigh drawn by reindeer.

Today Saint Nick, the jollier version of Father Christmas, is recalled in Fredericksburg on his feast day, December 6, or on the Saturday before, when the children are given a *Kinderfest* at the Pioneer Memorial Museum. They listen to stories, play games, decorate cookies, and hang their stockings over the large fireplace. Later they return to collect the treats Saint Nicholas leaves in the stockings.

Since 1979, the Fredericksburg Shopkeepers Guild has sponsored a Kristkindl Market, patterned after the famous Kristkindl Markets in Munich and Nuremberg. Costumed Jaycees hand out bags filled with

Ein glückliches
Neues Jahr

May Peace and Christmas
joys attend you
And Heaven its every
blessing send you

All Good Wishes for Christmas.

Joyful Christmas Greetings
Wishing you all the health and happiness
that one lifetime can hold, and also a
Merry Christmas

fruit and candy at the courthouse, and Saint Nicholas is seen strolling along Main Street.

Bethany Congregational Church in San Antonio preserves a very old German custom in *die deutsche Weihnachtsfeier* (Christmas Candlelight Service). In Germany a Christmas fair is traditionally held in the town square in front of the church on the night of the candlelighting. People gather from all over the community bringing lanterns with them. In the Candlelight Service sponsored by Bethany Church no sermon is preached in order to avoid doctrinal differences between Lutherans, "German Evangelicals," and Catholics. An ecumenical atmosphere is created wherein members of the whole German community and others may feel free to come together to celebrate a German Christmas on a community-wide basis.

The Christmas story is told in High German, which is used throughout the service. There are prayers and Bible readings and music by the San Antonio Liederkranz (established in 1892) or the Beethoven Männerchor (formed in 1867). The congregation joins in the singing of "Stille Nacht, Heilige Nacht" at the close of the service. Beautifully decorated with greenery and flowers, permeated with the sounds of the organ and carillon, and lighted with flickering candles, the church is the perfect setting for the majesty of a traditional German *Weihnachtsfeier.*

Traditionally, German families do not put up their Christmas tree until the day before Christmas, and then in a room kept closed to the children. The tree is decorated by the parents, presents are put under the tree, and the room is decorated. The aura of secrecy about the tree adds to the excitement. Some families go to Christmas Eve services, come home, and then open the room with the Christmas tree and presents, while other families wait until Christmas morning. German families who maintain strong ties to predominantly German communities and rural areas observe Saint Nicholas Day on December 6. The children are told stories about Saint Nicholas, and they hang stockings in hopes he will leave them treats such as candy, nuts, and a small gift or two.

One of the greatest contributions made to Christmas by the Germans is music. Two of the world's best-loved carols come to us from Germany. "Silent Night" was composed on Christmas Eve of 1818 in the little village of Obendorf in the Austrian Alps by the church minister and his organist. Because the church organ was broken, they wrote the simple carol to be sung to the accompaniment of a guitar, little dreaming that over 170 years later it would echo among the hills of Texas.

Many people sing the other perennial German favorite without knowing its message. The first two stanzas of "O Tannenbaum" ("O Christmas Tree") express delight in the steadfast nature of the evergreen that remains "faithful" throughout summer's heat and winter's ice and snow. And the last stanza pledges that the singer will learn to have the same qualities as the tree:

> O Christmas tree, O Christmas tree,
> Your leaves will teach me, also,
> That hope and love and faithfulness
> Are precious things I can possess.
> O Christmas tree, O Christmas tree,
> Your leaves will teach me, also.[8]

Wherever there was a German neighborhood of any size in Texas, a *Männerchor* (male chorus) was organized by a leader who had studied classical music. These meticulously trained groups have always been in great demand for performances at *Saengerfests* (singing festivals) and are especially popular during the Christmas season. From their homeland they brought such great music as Bach's "Christmas Oratorio" and Handel's *Messiah*. In San Antonio in December the Beethoven *Männerchor* and *Damenchor* (female chorus) perform concerts of sacred Christmas music.

December 26 is traditionally called Second Christmas by the Germans. Christmas Eve and the first Christmas Day require religious observances, but the second Christmas is the time when "young and old come out to play." Among the early German settlers in Texas it was a time for dances and public parties. Schottisches, waltzes (by German composers), and polkas were the most popular dances. Older people played games such as cards, dominoes, and pinochle. The custom of Second Christmas in Fredericksburg is preserved by members of the historical society who get together to sing and feast on German pioneer dishes. Other residents have adopted the habit of celebrating *Zweite Weihnachten* (Second Christmas) on the Sunday following Christmas—just to stretch the good times and good feelings of the season.

German oompah bands that play for dances and for entertainment at public events have always been enormously popular in Texas. In the 1850s Edward H. Cushing, editor of the Houston *Telegraph,* boasted that there was more Christmas spirit in the music of one Texas German band than in a whole orchestra in the city of Saint Louis.

A German immigrant, Louis Prang, is called the father of the American Christmas card. His cards, printed in eight to twenty colors by a process he invented, were treasured even in his own time. Although Christmas cards originated in England, Queen Victoria's daughter, the Crown Princess of Prussia, ordered her cards by cablegram from Louis Prang's publishing house near Boston.[9]

Credit also goes to German craftsmen for brightening Christmas for little girls since the middle of the nineteenth century. In *Children's Toys throughout the Ages* Leslie Daiken says: "By the year 1850, together with the Christmas tree and Easter Bunny, doll's tea-sets and dinner-services from Germany were capturing the imagination of all good little girls everywhere. They were faithful replicas. They were inexpensive and the pleasure to be derived from extending a collection little by little seemed boundless. Some sets were made of good porcelain—the majority of china-clay either rough or glazed. . . ."[10] The first commercial Christmas ornaments were made of tin by German tinsmiths, who also made tin doll dish sets. Glass tree ornaments evolved from the glass bead industry in Germany. As early as 1820 German glassblowers produced large, heavy balls covered with swirled colored wax and glass dust. Modern tree ornaments were created around 1870 by German glassblowers, and some were transported to Texas among the treasured household goods of German immigrants.

From the time of the earliest German settlers in Texas, it has been their custom to keep open house during the week from Christmas to New Year's with a constant round of visiting and eating. The greeting "Come to our tree" always means refreshments will be served. German housewives brought recipes from Germany that had been handed down from generation to generation. Many of the recipes are for cookies that improve with time and so can be made well in advance of the holiday season.

German women quickly learned to substitute native Texas pecans for the hazelnuts and walnuts used by their ancestors in the old country. After the nuts were gathered, families spent long fall evenings cracking them and picking out the meats for Christmas baking. Weeks in advance the family made the Christmas cookies that would hang on the tree, using special dough and cookie cutters reserved for this occasion. The cutters, usually handmade, came in various symbolic shapes —hearts to show Christ's love for mankind, stars to recall the star of Bethlehem, candles to portray the light Christ brought to the world, the Christian fish, and doves, lambs, ducks, horses, bells, Christmas trees, toys, butterflies, flowers, and Saint Nicholas. Many of these forms are still used. Gilbert Jordan remembers decorating Christmas cookies as one of the most enjoyable pre-Christmas activities. His entire family gathered around the dining table to decorate the cookies: "They were first covered with a layer of white icing, then with colored icing we drew all kinds of designs on them . . . or we strewed colored sugar and other decorations on the fresh icings."[11]

The Timmermann sisters' collection of cookie cutters fills several very large cannisters. Some of these were used by the girls in the orphanage, and some were made by a local tinsmith from designs created by the sisters. The shapes of the cookie cutters include poinsettias, rocking horses, candy canes, and a church with windowpanes to color. The cookies they make for their famous tree are from a recipe in their great-grandmother's cookbook dating from 1840.

Timmermann Sisters' Christmas Cookies

½ lb. butter   3 eggs
1 lb. sugar   1 lb. flour

Cream butter, and add sugar. Add eggs one at a time. Beat well. Add enough flour so dough can be rolled on board. Cut out. Use a wooden pick or skewer end to make holes in cookies so tree hangers can be attached. Bake at 350° for 12–15 minutes. Cool on wire rack. Makes about 3½ dozen cookies. The cookies can be kept in the freezer from year to year to use as decorations.

The sisters decorate the cookies with an icing made with powdered sugar, flour, and water. Using egg white for glue, they decorate the cookies with assorted colored sugar crystals, red and green candied cherries, bits

of cedar greenery, chocolate shot, and gold and silver dragées. If some of the cookies are intended for eating, they add fruits and nuts and vanilla flavoring to the dough.

By 1963 the Timmermann sisters had achieved such fame that they were asked to become cookie bakers to the U.S. president. The German ambassador was visiting the Johnson farm home on the Pedernales, and President Johnson wanted special cookies for the tree. The sisters went to work. They made cookies in amusing shapes for Luci and Linda, a Papa Johnson cookie for the president, a cardinal for Lady Bird, a figure representing the visiting ambassador, and a U.S. map cookie.

Germans generally ate goose for Christmas. However, as happened with other European immigrants, Germans gradually exchanged their traditional Christmas goose for the more readily available Texas wild turkey. But the custom of eating herring salad at Christmas and New Year's for good luck remains popular. The salad varies with handed-down recipes, but it usually contains a mixture of boiled smoked diced herring, mixed with beets, hard-boiled eggs, pickles, apples, potatoes, and vinegar. Sometimes other smoked meats such as veal or beef are added. Sausages and pork in various dishes and dark yeast breads are featured at German holiday meals.

The coffee pot was always on, and homemade cake and wine were offered to guests. The wine was made from mustang grapes or agarita berries or whatever fruit was available. Because German tradition held that *Lebkuchen* (honey cakes) sustained life, they were often given to the poor at Christmas.

Always sure to be on hand in German homes was *Weihnachtsstollen*, or Christmas bread. This is a yeast bread that has raisins, candied fruit, and chopped almonds or other nuts in it, with an icing of powdered sugar and milk. While it is still hot, the thin icing is brushed on, and it may be decorated with fruit or nuts.

Springerle cookies, or anise cookies, are also popular Christmas treats. They can be made with aniseed or anise extract. *Pfeffernuesse* (peppernut) cookies are also sure to be found in German homes during the holidays.

Marzipan, a sweet as pleasing to the eye as to the taste, gives the German cook an opportunity to be an artist. The basic dough is made by mixing almond paste with egg whites and confectioners' sugar. It is

Lebkuchen
Esther L. Bray

1 cup honey
1 egg, well beaten
grated rind of 1 lemon
2 T. lemon juice
⅔ cup packed dark brown sugar
½ cup finely chopped almonds
½ cup minced citron

2¼ cups flour
1 t. cinnamon
½ t. each ground cloves, mace,
    allspice, nutmeg, soda, salt
blanched slivered almonds
    (optional)
slivered citron (optional)

Heat honey just under boiling point in a saucepan. Cool to lukewarm. Add egg, lemon rind, lemon juice, and brown sugar. Mix almonds and citron with ¼ cup flour. Mix remaining flour with spices, soda, and salt in large mixing bowl. Combine honey mixture with dry ingredients. Add almond and citron mixture, and mix with hands. Cover bowl with foil, and refrigerate for at least 12 hours. Divide dough in quarters, and roll each into a 6×4½-inch rectangle. With pastry wheel, cut into six 3×½-inch cookies. Place on greased baking sheet, 2 inches apart, and spread with glaze. Decorate with blanched almond halves and thin slivers of citron, or leave plain. Put in 400° oven, reduce heat at once to 375° and bake 15–20 minutes or until cookies just test done. Do not bake until hard and dry; these should be chewy and moist.

GLAZE

1 egg white
⅔ cup confectioners' sugar

dash of salt
¼ t. vanilla or lemon juice

Beat egg white until stiff. Fold in sugar, salt, and vanilla or lemon juice. (Note: sometimes the cookies are baked without glazing or they are glazed after baking, especially if they are to be decorated for Christmas gifts.)

shaped to resemble fruits: apples, bananas, pears, apricots, cherries, or strawberries. A glaze made with sugar and water is poured over the fruit shapes and they are allowed to dry overnight. The artistry comes in shaping and coloring the dough. Drops of food color suitable to the kind of fruit are added. Then cloves are added for apple stems, brown food color (made by mixing basic colors) is painted in characteristic lines on bananas, leaves of dried rosemary are used as pear leaves, and so on. Stored in tightly covered containers, the candy will keep several weeks. But it is too pretty to hide away and so usually does not last long.

In 1896 a master German baker, August Weidmann, formed a part-

Pfeffernuesse
Esther L. Bray

3 eggs	2 t. cinnamon
2 cups packed light brown sugar	½ t. freshly ground black pepper
2 cups flour	1 cup finely chopped almonds
½ t. baking powder	1 box (15 oz.) seedless raisins, ground
½ t. soda	2 T. ground citron
½ t. salt	confectioners' sugar
1 t. ground cloves	

Beat eggs and brown sugar until light. Sift flour with baking powder, soda, salt, cloves, cinnamon, and pepper into large bowl. Add almonds, raisins, and citron to dry ingredients, and stir to coat. Pour egg-sugar mixture into flour-spice mixture, and stir to make stiff dough. Using 1 rounded teaspoonful of dough at a time, roll into balls between floured palms. (If dough is too sticky to shape, chill 1 hour or longer.) Put on well-greased baking sheet, leaving 2-inch spaces between cookies to allow for spreading. Bake at 375° for 10–12 minutes or until cookies hold their shape. Do not cook hard or dry. They should be moist inside because they dry out as time goes by. While still warm, roll well in confectioners' sugar, or shake with sugar in a brown paper bag. When cool, store airtight. These cookies should be stored at least a week before being eaten. Makes 4 dozen.

nership with W. T. McElwee and began a bakery in Corsicana. Using the recipe for *weiss kuchen mit frucht* (fruitcake), which he had brought from Wiesbaden, he created "DeLuxe Fruitcakes." The cakes became famous, and the bakery has been visited by such notable fans as Will Rogers, Enrico Caruso, and John Ringling. Although the partners have died, Gus Weidmann's recipe still hangs on a clipboard in the kitchen, and the bakery continues each holiday season to receive orders to fill gift lists from European royalty, famous American novelists, movie stars, and hundreds of ordinary folks.

Hermann Seele, the German immigrant who described his visit to the Ervendberg orphanage so vividly, has also left us a touching recollection of his first Christmas in Texas. He had arrived in Galveston only a week earlier, and on Christmas Eve he went first to the Methodist church. But the pastor there preached "too loudly and too rapidly," so Seele "betook" himself to the Episcopal church, where the solemn, full-voiced singing of the familiar "Glory to God in the Highest" soothed him. After the service he walked along the deserted beach, "a lonely stranger in a country still so new to me." The skies, the sea, and the land seemed gray and murky. But then the moon broke through the cloud bank, transforming the scene:

> As it had for thousands of years, the moon flooded its mother, the earth, with reflected sunlight. Before me now lay the broad sea as though encircled by a halo. It formed a bridge of light over which my thoughts traveled to the distant, familiar scene with my loved ones in the old homeland and up to the radiant, heavenly heights of eternal love. And, amidst the roar of the surf, from my soul that was deeply stirred and my heart that was filled with joy there came forth the words:
>
> > Glory be to God in the highest,
> > Peace on Earth,
> > And good will to men.[12]

CHRISTMAS GREETINGS
May all the years' memory of wonderful days
Lead up to this day of Christmas pleasure,
With its joys and its hopes of things to come
In a New Year of bountiful measure.

Leo and Lillian

A Dickens of a Christmas:

THE HERITAGE FROM THE BRITISH ISLES

Happy Christmas! There is an often repeated story of a young girl's reaction when Charles Dickens died. "Is Mr. Dickens dead?" she asked with tears in her eyes. "And will Father Christmas die, too?"

Dickens, who was sometimes himself called Father Christmas, immortalized in his Christmas books and in *The Pickwick Papers* the rich traditions associated with an English Yuletide. Early in December each year, the Strand in Galveston becomes the London Strand as it was in Victorian times. During "Dickens on the Strand" hundreds of costumed characters bring to life a nineteenth-century Christmas celebration. Beefeaters and bobbies, town criers, jugglers, carolers, and dozens of Dickens's creations roam the streets. Scrooge is followed by the ghosts of Christmas Past, Christmas Present, and Christmas Yet to Come. Pickwick, Tiny Tim, Miss Havisham, Fagin, David Copperfield, ruffians, and pickpockets share in the merrymaking. Even Queen Victoria unbends and smiles as she surveys the scene from her royal coach. Top-hatted vendors sell 'ot chestnuts for a few pence, and various vendors and shops offer handmade toys, nosegays, old-fashioned tree ornaments, spice balls made of oranges or apples studded with cloves, and other Victorian trinkets and treasures. Entertainment includes a performance of *A Christmas Carol,* mimes, story telling, a performing bear, and Punch and Judy shows. In the Covent Garden open-air market, hungry visitors can sample plum pudding, treacle tarts, pork pies, syllabub, wassail, and other tempting foods and beverages. Pubs called the Half Moon Tap and the Elephant and Castle offer mulled cider, eggnog, port, and sherry. This lavish spectacle, which began in 1974, is a reminder of the many holiday traditions brought to Texas by the British.

Early immigrants from England, Ireland, Scotland, and Wales came to Texas by two routes. Some made their way overland by wagon and horseback, crossing the Red River or the Louisiana border, often after having lived several years in other states. Other English-speaking settlers came directly from their homeland to Texas by boat, arriving at Galveston or Velasco or other ports on the Gulf before making their way inland. English and Scottish empresarios were not notably successful in settling large groups in Texas. However, ranching, land investment, and other business opportunities attracted individuals and small groups of English and Scots, who tended to disperse and become assimilated into the Anglo-American communities. Irish empresarios were more successful, and the 1860 Texas census lists almost thirty-five hundred Irish. The Welsh did not settle in Texas in large groups, but native Welshmen died at the Alamo. And an extraordinary Welshman, Morgan Jones, built West Texas' railway system and became president of the Fort Worth and Denver City Railway.

Among the seasonal customs brought to Texas by the British was keeping the Twelve Days of Christmas. With this custom came a version of an old counting carol dating back to medieval times. With a few changes it has become the popular "Twelve Days of Christmas." Originally the four calling birds were "colly" birds (probably meaning coal-black birds). Instead of seven swans there were seven squabs swimming; eight maids milking were eight hounds running. Nine bears were "a-beating" instead of nine ladies dancing; ten cocks were crowing instead of ten lords leaping. There were eleven leaping lords in the old version, but they have been replaced by eleven pipers piping. And there were twelve ladies dancing instead of twelve drummers drumming.

Today Austin has a "Twelve Nights of a Capital Christmas" celebration. There are nightly musical performances in the Capitol rotunda, and various businesses offer free refreshments, balloons, and entertainment. On the sixth night (geese-a-laying), the Austin Crest Hotel offers a Christmas egg hunt. On the eleventh night (pipers piping), the *Austin American-Statesman* provides Scottish dancing accompanied by bagpipes and drums. And on the twelfth night, Santa Claus arrives. The way he will arrive remains a secret up until the last minute. His transportation has ranged from a trusty steed to a red convertible, and it is always a surprise.

The twelve days of celebration in Britain began with the ritual of bringing in the Yule log and ended with the extinguishing of the log, while carefully saving a fagot to light the next year's log. Certain super-stitions were attached to the ritual. The log was lighted with a fagot saved from the year before lest the house burn down. It had to ignite the first time lest trouble follow and was kept burning for twelve hours lest ill luck come. It acquired the tradition that it burned away old ha-treds and misunderstandings, and it might be blessed or "toasted" by pouring wine or brandy on it. The ashes of the Yule log were thought to give fertility to the ground, rid cattle of vermin, and cure toothaches.

Nineteenth-century Texas plantations, ranches, and towns observed the tradition of bringing in the Yule log. Ralph Semmes Jackson re-membered that one of the first preparations for the Christmas festivities on his East Texas ranch was to cut and haul a Yule log to put into the six-foot fireplace. The log, which had to burn from Christmas to New Year's, was a section of the trunk of an oak tree. It was about five feet long and between two and three feet thick, and a block and tackle was used to skid the log up boards laid on the back steps. Then the log was rolled along boards into the fireplace and pushed into place against the back wall. A fire of smaller logs, built in front of the backlog, gradually burned it away, and each morning coals from the backlog were used to start the fire again. In 1966 Austin's Parks and Recreation Department initiated the city's "first annual" Yulefest with the ceremonial lighting of a giant Yule log in Zilker Park. Today, the Yule log burns in Zilker Park from December 3–21.

There are many legends concerning the origin of the Christmas tree. One tells that the English missionary Saint Boniface saw the first Christmas tree when he stopped a pagan sacrifice in Germany. After Boniface chopped down the oak beneath which the sacrifice was taking place, a young fir appeared in its place. Boniface told the people the fir was the tree of life, representing Christ.

Decorated Christmas trees arrived in England in 1844 when Prince Albert, Queen Victoria's German husband, had one set up at Windsor Castle for their children. The *London Illustrated Times* published a picture of it. As the royal family went, so went the nation, and soon Christmas trees replaced Yule logs in importance. The Victorians elaborated on the simply decorated German tree, adding fanciful ornaments, pretty pictures from their scrapbooks, tinsel, angel hair, knitted objects, and chains made of paper and other materials, as well as decorated paper cones filled with goodies. English immigrants to Texas after the middle of the nineteenth century brought along the idea of a more elaborately decorated tree.

The British tradition of using holly, ivy, and mistletoe for holiday decorating has many myths and legends connected with it. In English carols the holly represents the male and the ivy the female spirit. Holly is associated with the wood of the cross and the crown of thorns; its use as a Christmas decoration probably came about because of its appropriate color and timing. A lonely Englishman, living on a Texas border ranch, recalled keeping the Christmas fiesta with his Mexican workers, but "not without memories of other Christmas days, so different from these, and distant friends and holly-decked churches in far-off England."[1] Superstitions about ivy have to do with preventing drunkenness and promoting fertility. And an Irish belief is that an ivy leaf placed in water in a covered dish between New Year's and Old Christmas (January 6) will foretell the future. If the leaf remains green, good health is forecast, but if it becomes spotted, sickness and death will follow.

Finding mistletoe growing plentifully in Texas, British settlers used it in their decorating, combining it with greenery to make a "kissing bough." Mistletoe was regarded as a sacred plant by the Celtic Druids, and sprigs of it were hung over doors to ward off evil spirits and to ensure fertility. Perhaps this has something to do with the license to kiss under its boughs. In *The Pickwick Papers,* Dickens promoted the idea by describing a delightful kissing spree at Dingley Dell:

> As to the poor relations, they kissed everybody, not excepting the plain portions of the young-lady visitors, who in their excessive confusion, ran right under the mistletoe, as soon as it was hung up, without knowing it!
>
> Mr. Pickwick was standing under the mistletoe looking with a very pleased countenance on all that was passing around him, when the young lady with the black eyes, after a little whispering with the other young ladies, made a sudden dart forward, and putting her arms around Mr. Pickwick's neck, saluted him affectionately on the left cheek; and before Mr. Pickwick distinctly knew what was the matter, he was surrounded by the whole body, and kissed by everyone of them.[2]

This custom quickly caught on in nineteenth-century Texas, where kissing needed more of an excuse than it does today.

Recently mistletoe has also become big business around the Christmas holidays. Today ninety-five percent of the world's supply of mistletoe is produced in a twelve-county area in Central Texas. During the first two weeks in December half a million pounds of mistletoe are removed from mesquite, oak, blackjack, chinaberry, and other trees and graded, packed, and shipped throughout the world.

Lighted candles are a Christmas symbol used in many European countries. In medieval times a burning candle represented Christ, a tradition preserved in many church liturgies. In the history of Ireland, the Christmas candles took on additional significance. Under English Protestant persecution, priests hid in forests and caves and visited farms and homes secretly to say mass at night. At Christmastime the Irish placed candles in their windows hoping to guide priests to their houses. But they told the English soldiers that the candles were there to guide Mary and Joseph to a place where they could stay. The Irish kept the custom after the need for it had passed, and it evolved into placing candles within wreaths of holly or laurel to burn throughout Holy Night.

Among Christmas decorations today in Texas, many wreathed candles can be seen in windows.

Before the English Civil War, Saint Nicholas was so revered in Britain that many Anglican churches were named in his honor. After the no-frills Puritans outlawed him from England in the seventeenth century, he returned to England sometime during the Victorian period disguised as Father Christmas, riding on a goat or a donkey. In Texas, as in the rest of the United States, he evolved into the familiar red-suited Santa and acquired eight reindeer to provide power for his sleigh, with Rudolph as guide in more recent times. Father Christmas was never accompanied by the threatening companions other European gift givers were, but was always a dearly beloved, kindly grandfather figure.

Christmas cards developed in England from the popular Valentine's cards in vogue there in the mid-nineteenth century. After the royal family began sending Christmas cards, and with the introduction of the penny post in 1840, the custom of sending season's greetings to one's friends—and customers—became widespread. In the 1880s Prang and Company of Boston began to promote the idea of sending Christmas cards in the United States. The idea quickly caught on in Texas, and cards with Texas motifs such as cactus, oil wells, and roadrunners became popular. Individuals and businesses annually sent out thousands of cards, but the recent introduction of the twenty-five-cent first-class postage rate has caused a drop in the number of cards sent.

The British also brought to Texas the custom of playing Yuletide games. Riddling, which usually involved some aspect of British life, did not translate well in pioneer Texas. But the more active British games, and especially tournaments patterned after those of the Age of Chivalry, became a highlight of the season in many West Texas towns following the American Civil War. Large crowds gathered on the edge of the towns to watch the local cowboys become knights. Wearing elaborate costumes featuring silver-trimmed black shirts and trousers and topped with wide-brimmed hats with plumes, these transformed cowboys assumed such names as Morning Star and Black Warrior. The ceremonies began with a grand parade led by a marshal, followed by the knights on their best-bedecked horses. The contests were run on a hundred-yard course, with five posts set about fifteen yards apart. A steel ring attached to a wire by a clothespin hung from a crossbar on each post.

The contestants had ten seconds to ride down the course and try to spear the rings with their long, spiked steel lances. Each rider ran the course three times, and the one spearing the most rings won. One of the prizes was the winner's right to choose the queen for the coronation ball.

The holiday season was a time for transplanted Brits to recall what they had left behind. One remedy for nostalgic yearnings was to try to follow the old traditions in their new homes. Some were more successful than others in recreating the customs they remembered. William Hughes, a young homesick Englishman, found himself on a small sheep ranch on the Rio Grande on Christmas Day of 1878. Datelining his letter "Guinagato Ranche, 20 miles from Anywhere, Texas," he described his disastrous Christmas Day to his family back in England:

> We had an awful day, and were out of provisions and corn and every-thing, and nearly got frozen. . . . 5 A.M. got up from under wagon and found icicles all about. It was raining, everything was wet, sheep had stampeded and were at last found in three different places some miles off, and brought back by three of the others nearly at night. X–– and I started in the middle of the day on horseback for the nearest ranche to get corn for the houses. It was awful cold and rain-ing, and we thought we had lost our way, but at last we heard the roosters crowing and got to the ranche, where we thawed and had coffee and "muscal," or brandy made from cactus. Then we started back and dried the blankets and things as well as possible in a rain. . . . We had killed a wild pig, and had intended to have boar's head for Christmas dinner . . . but unfortunately a dog ran off with the head.[3]

Mary J. Jaques, a spirited Englishwoman who experimented with ranching near Junction, was more successful in combining the old ways with the new to produce a satisfactory celebration of the season. When December temperatures in Junction rose to ninety degrees, she found it hard to realize that the cakes, plum puddings, and mincemeat pies they were making "were actually intended for Christmas." On Christ-mas, after a feast that included turkey and roast suckling pig, they at-tended horse races and competitions. Mary had a keen eye for detail:

> At two o'clock began the races, of an amusingly nondescript char-acter—horses, ponies of all ages and sizes, carrying any weight, and

ridden with or without saddle, as the case might be. "Lifting the rings," afforded an opportunity to display some neat horsemanship, but our champion had drunk not wisely, but too well, and actually seeing double, remained under the impression that he had all the rings on his pole, when there was but one. . . .

Another dexterous feat is to pick up a hat, a handkerchief, or even a dollar, from the ground at full gallop.

Mary had wanted to enter the ladies' race herself, but it fell through because there were too few entries. Holding to her native habits, she served tea after the races. Then there was a fireworks display. "The fame of our Roman candles, rockets and fire-balloons spread in due course as far as San Antonio," she reported. Unfortunately, the fireworks set the roof of the gallery on fire. A bucket brigade made up of neighbors extinguished the fire. Following that excitement, the family went to a dance at the courthouse in Junction. "Cowboys," Mary observed, "are not exactly light-footed, but they are very springy." And she noted that they were extremely particular about their "high-heeled shoes," which must have fine uppers and "fit like a glove."[4]

Adult Scots have traditionally focused on children on Christmas but have reserved Hogmanay (New Year's Eve) for themselves. They brought to Texas their beloved Hogmanay superstitions and customs, including unbounded hospitality and glorious gluttony. Between Christmas and Hogmanay they turn their houses upside down making them spotless for the New Year. No dish must be unwashed, no garment dirty or unmended, and no speck of last year's dust must be found at the stroke of midnight on December 31. Their tables laden with black bun, cherry cake, shortbread, plus assorted bottles, they peer eagerly from behind their clean curtains to see who will "first foot" their homes. The first foot, or first person to cross the threshold after midnight on Hogmanay, will determine the fortune of the house in the New Year. If a tall, dark man carrying coal or a full bottle appears, good luck is assured. But a redhead, especially a woman, brings dread of dire events to follow. Lately, peppermint chocolates or a sprig of evergreen have been considered acceptable substitutes for the coal.

The Scottish tradition of unstinting hospitality fitted in with the pattern of life in pioneer Texas, but some of their best-loved holiday foods never really caught on. The Scots eat black bun on "Ne'er Day"

(New Year Day) for good luck. This peculiar delicacy was described in medieval times as being spices and fruit in a pastry "coffyne." It is a solid and spicy sort of fruitcake baked in a pie crust and may be oblong or round. The Scots also brought along their recipes for haggis, which has been called their national dish and dubbed "Great chieftain o' the puddin' race" by Robert Burns. Made from calf or sheep hearts, livers, lungs, and small intestines, boiled in the animal's stomach, haggis is traditionally served with neeps, tatties, and nips (mashed turnips, mashed potatoes, and nips of whiskey).

Some of the delicious sweets offered by the Scottish settlers were undoubtedly more pleasing to the taste of their Texas neighbors. These include Scottish trifle, which comes in many variations and allows cooks to use their creativity. This showy dessert is made by laying slices of sponge cake in a deep glass dish, spreading preserves between the slices, and heaping the dish with whipped cream or a rich custard sauce, to which brandy has been added. Other favorites are scones and the famous Scottish shortbread.

Tea Scones

2 cups flour
¼ cup butter
1 t. baking powder
¼ t. salt

2 T. sugar
2 T. raisins
1 egg
½ cup milk

Place flour in a bowl; rub in butter. Add baking powder, salt, sugar, and raisins. Mix well. Beat egg, and add to milk; reserve 1 tablespoon of mixture. Add remainder to dry ingredients. Knead to make moist dough. Turn onto well-floured board. Roll out ¾-inch thick. Cut into 2-inch rounds with biscuit cutter. Arrange on lightly floured baking sheet. Brush tops with reserved egg mixture. Bake at 425° until risen and lightly browned, about 25 minutes. Let cool. Makes 9.

Shortbread is often decorated with sugared almonds and candied orange or citron peel and sent as a gift at Christmas and Hogmanay. It is sinfully rich, as it is made with the freshest, sweetest, best butter, never margarine. The version in this book, an old Ayrshire recipe, is easy enough for beginners and rewarding enough for experienced cooks.

Shortbread

1 cup butter	¼ t. salt
½ cup light brown sugar	¼ t. baking powder
2 cups flour	

Cream butter and sugar. Sift together flour, salt, and baking powder. Add to butter mixture, and mix well. Roll out ½-inch thick, and cut in rounds or squares. For petticoat tails, cut into a large round using a plate as a guide, then cut a smaller round in the center. Divide the larger circle into eighths. Remove to cookie sheet, leaving ½-inch spaces between triangles. Prick with a fork. Bake at 325° for 20 minutes or until lightly browned. Sprinkle with sugar as soon as they are removed from oven. Cool a little before lifting from baking sheet. Makes 16–24 cookies.

A Welsh dish that is handy for quick holiday lunches or suppers is the ever-popular Welsh Rarebit (Caws-Wedi-Pobi).

Welsh Rarebit

4 slices toast	1 t. dry mustard
½ lb. cheese	2 t. flour
1 t. butter	4 T. milk or beer
2 t. Worcestershire sauce	salt and pepper

Toast bread. Grate cheese into a saucepan, and heat gently until melted. Add remaining ingredients, and mix well. Spread over toast and return to grill until brown. (Instead of pre-cooking cheese mixture, grated cheese and seasonings can be mixed with enough additional milk to give a spreadable mixture, piled on toast, and then heated under grill. Garnish with parsley, and serve at once.)

An Irish contribution to a festive holiday is Irish coffee, which may be served as an after-dinner drink or as a dessert. To serve one person, put one tablespoon of brown sugar in the bottom of a cup or stemmed glass. Add one and a half ounces of Irish whiskey, and fill the cup with hot coffee. Top with whipped cream, flavored with sugar and vanilla.

Sir Walter Scott described wassail bowls decorated with ribbons, and Dickens praised the "mighty bowl of wassail in which the hot apples hissed and bubbled." Long before the time of these writers, however, carolers in Merrie Olde England sang:

> Wassail, wassail, all over town
> Our toast it is white
> And our ale it is brown.

In return for the coins tossed to them, they drank to the health of the donors. Early versions of wassail were made of ale and had toast floating on top, so the drinkers were said to "toast" their benefactors.

Drinking to the health (or thriving) of inanimate things—such as "wassailing the apple trees"—is a very old English custom. But it is dour, cold Henry VII who gets credit for introducing the Scandinavian custom of the wassail bowl into England. And it is his pleasure-loving son, Henry VIII, who incorporated it into a lengthy holiday period of rollicking gluttony.

The royal Christmas feast at Henry VIII's court began at three in the afternoon and lasted past midnight. Hundreds of servants prepared and served the meal, which was introduced with a parade led by the Lord High Steward on horseback. The chief cook, carrying a roasted boar's head, followed. After him came two men staggering under the weight of the huge wassail bowl. The wooden bowl, filled with hot ale and spices, fitted into a heavy, richly embossed silver holder. The religious significance of the season was marked by twelve crab apples floating in the bowl, representing the twelve apostles. Three cloves stuck in each apple represented the Trinity. In addition to wassail, various wines and mead flowed freely during the meal, which included brawn (headcheese), roast peacock, and mutton pies. From the mutton pies developed mince pies, which were originally baked in the shape of a manger. Puddings of all kinds—such as fish pudding, blood pudding, suet pudding, and plum pudding—were popular. Part of the entertainment was to douse the suet and plum puddings with spiced wine and set them afire.

Wassail bowls at festive holiday gatherings are probably even more popular today than they were in the nineteenth century. Punches made with cider and rum are often called "wassails," and nobody seems to mind.

Eggnog, whiskey punch, syllabub, and homemade wine were the holiday drinks most often mentioned in pioneer Texas. William Bollaert noted that Christmas Day was greeted with "egg nogs, the favourite beverage this morning (made of the white and yellow of eggs, beaten up separately, the yellow with sugar, then both mixed with whiskey, brandy and new milk to thin it)—somewhat pleasant, but of a bilious nature."[7] Bollaert, like many other people, may have believed eggnogs originated in our southern states, but they are mentioned as far back as the seventeenth century in England and are probably a descendant of the English sack posset, a hot drink made with ale or sack (dry Spanish wine). Thick eggnogs were believed to be good for invalids.

Syllabub is similar to eggnog, except that it is made with wine. Depending on its consistency, syllabub may be drunk like eggnog, eaten with a spoon as a light dessert, or spooned over cake. Special syllabub churns and egg beaters as well as delicate goblets and bowls that were used on Texas plantations still exist in private homes and in museums. The goblets and serving bowl were often of such pretty colors and designs that they were kept on display on sideboards. Early recipes called for making syllabub "under the cow" by putting the bowl containing wine sweetened with sugar under a cow and milking into it until there was "a fine froth on top." Not surprisingly, milkmaids were reported to be fond of syllabub. A syllabub recipe not requiring the presence of a cow calls for two cups of whipping cream, one-half cup of whole milk, one-half cup of sugar, and one-half cup of sherry whipped together.

An old English superstition says that to refuse mince pie is to court bad luck for the following year. Another warns that you will lose a friend before the next Christmas if you don't partake of holiday plum pudding. And a third assures that those who get a piece of the pudding while it is still flaming will get their wishes. Traditionally, fortune-telling objects are baked into the pudding: a dime signifies money; a ring forecasts love; but a button or a thimble means the finder will remain unmarried. A recipe brought over by an English family, that of Mrs. H. H. Sharpe, has been used for over a hundred and fifty years in Texas.

Renaissance Boar's Head festivals seem to be an emerging tradition in Texas. Churches, such as the University Christian Church in Fort

Plum Pudding
Mrs. H. H. Sharpe

1 lb. grated bread crumbs
   (use stale bread)
1 lb. suet (beef kidney suet,
   chopped finely)
1 lb. brown sugar
1 t. cinnamon
1 t. nutmeg
2 cups pecans, chopped
1 lb. currants

1 box lemon peel, chopped finely
½ lb. citron, chopped finely
2 lemons (juice and grated rind)
1 lb. raisins
½ lb. candied cherries, chopped
½ lb. candied pineapple, chopped
8 eggs
1 cup whiskey (100 proof)

Put bread crumbs, suet, and sugar in a pan with spices, and mix well. Add pecans and currants; mix again. Add grated lemon peel and citron. Pour lemon juice over this, and mix well. Add raisins, cherries, and pineapple; mix well again. Add well-beaten eggs and whiskey; mix again. If not moist enough, add a little beer or strong coffee. Mixture should be very moist, but should not have any extra liquid. Pack in greased molds, firmly but not tightly. Cover with cloths, and put on rack in pot over 1 inch of boiling water, and steam for 4 hours. When ready to serve, steam pudding for 1 hour to reheat. To serve, unmold on warm platter, cover with warm brandy, and ignite. Serve with hard sauce. Makes 16–20 servings.

HARD SAUCE

1 stick soft butter
¾ cup powdered sugar
¼ cup sifted flour

2 cups half-and-half
1 t. vanilla
½ cup warm whiskey

In top of double boiler, cream butter, powdered sugar, and flour. Add half-and-half and vanilla. Heat, but do not boil. Just before serving, add whiskey.

Worth, and various college drama or music departments annually stage elaborate Boar's Head festivals featuring beefeaters, sprites and elves, wise men, shepherds, court ladies and gentlemen, and jesters. There is singing and dancing with madrigals and other traditional music. And the highlight of the ceremony is a parade during which the boar's head is brought in on a large silver platter surrounded by holly and fruit. The boar's head then becomes the centerpiece of the feast that follows.

Today at Hillingdon, a Texas ranch started by Englishman Alfred Giles (one of Texas' most distinguished nineteenth-century architects), the boar's head centerpiece is replaced by a deer's head complete with antlers, adorned with strings of cranberries. This custom originated when the English settlers found it easier to bag a deer than a boar in the Texas Hill Country. Another convenient substitution was agarita jelly instead of cranberry jelly.

Along with their treasured recipes for plum pudding, the English and Scots brought along some elaborate silver services which are still in use today. At Braehead Ranch near Boerne, the Christmas feast is still served on the "twenty-four of everything" set of silverware brought over by the founders of the ranch. And the flaming plum pudding arrives on the same grand pudding plate, complete with heavy silver cover, that has been used by the family for generations.

It would be hard for Texans to imagine Christmas without the old familiar English carols. Until the fourteenth century in England the word *carol* (from *carolare*) was associated with ring dances accompanied by singing. The following are only a few of the many Christmas songs that came to Texas from Britain. "Adeste Fideles" ("O Come, All Ye Faithful") has only recently been discovered to have been written by an Englishman, J. F. Wade, between 1740 and 1745. "The First Nowell," one of the oldest of the ballad carols, probably originated in Cornwall. In *A Christmas Carol*, Scrooge, before his reformation, was driven into a frenzy by the repetition of the carol "God Rest Ye Merry, Gentlemen." "Deck the Halls" is a lively Welsh carol. "Greensleeves," a love song from Elizabethan times (which Shakespeare used in several plays) supplied the tune for "What Child Is This?" Nahum Tate, an English poet laureate, wrote "While Shepherds Watched Their Flocks by Night" as a musical rendering of chapter 2 of the Gospel of Saint Luke, verses 8–15. The text of "Joy to the World" is from Isaac Watts's adaptation of Psalm 98. And the traditional "We Wish You a Merry Christmas" is probably the most often repeated of the English carols today—thanks to its adoption by the business world for use in interminable commercials.

For Texas and the rest of the English-speaking world, Scotland's supreme contribution to the emotional flavor of the season is Robert Burns's "Auld Lang Syne." Most people think they know at least the chorus. But Scots cringe when they hear the dreaded "zyne" instead of the sibilant "syne" (since; ago), or when "for the sake of" is gratuitously bellowed as part of the last line. The correct words of the chorus as printed in the Edinburgh *Scotsman* (December 31, 1979) are:

> For auld lang syne, my dear
> For auld lang syne,
> We'll take a cup o' kindness yet
> For auld lang syne!

Marley's ghost in Dickens's *A Christmas Carol* is probably the best-known Christmas ghost, but the British have a number of folklore beliefs connected with ghosts at Christmastime. One is that if someone opens a door to the house on Christmas Eve just as the clock strikes twelve, all ghosts will run out of the house. Also, the ringing of bells frightens ghosts away, which is why hand bell ringers accompany groups of carolers. But those born on Christmas need not fear ghosts, for they will be able to see ghosts and order them around. A Scottish superstition is that fires should not be allowed to go out on Christmas Eve lest ghosts or bad elves come down the chimney and dance in the cold ashes.

British customs—stories, carols, games, Yule logs, holly, mistletoe, food, and drinks—have become thoroughly assimilated into Texas holiday celebrations. Today it is difficult to know which were brought here directly from the British Isles and which came in with Anglo-American descendants of earlier British immigrants. But one thing is certain. The British people, like the reformed Ebenezer Scrooge of *A Christmas Carol*, know "how to keep Christmas well."

Narodil se Ježíšek,
kópíme mu kožíšek
hodně dlóhé, chlopaté,
abe ho měl na pate.

zHané

Kolaches, Polkas, and Blessed Chalk:

THE CZECH HERITAGE

Veselé Vánoce! Texas Czechs are noted for their habits of hard work, their tasty food, and their love of any kind of celebration, including community picnics, weddings, festivals, Saturday night dances, songfests, and holidays. Czech immigration to Texas in the last fifteen years has caused a renewal of Czech traditions. Their wholehearted celebration of the Christmas season satisfies both body and spirit.

A modern Czech Christmas parody combines parts of "'Twas the Night before Christmas" with parts of "Rudolph the Red-Nosed Reindeer." The poem begins with the stillness of the "haus" where not even a "maus" is stirring. After Santa arrives and Rudolph get stuck on the roof, the pragmatic Czech solution is to put tire chains on his feet to get him moving again. At the end of the poem Santa says, "We thank you very much. We wish you a Merry Christmas and to all a good night."[1] This poem illustrates the Czechs' ability to take what they find and with imagination and humor make it peculiarly their own. Combining these traits with their innate pride and determination, Czech Texans have kept alive their language and their culture, including their cherished Christmas customs.

Although adventurous Czechs began wandering into Texas as early as the 1820s, it wasn't until the 1850s that large groups of immigrants from the traditional major Czech homelands of Bohemia (*Čechy*), Moravia, and Slovakia settled in enclaves across a wide belt of Texas.[2] The religious heritage of the Czechs who came to Texas is somewhat complicated, but most were Catholic or Protestant, and they all brought along treasured traditions.

Like other European immigrants, Czechs celebrate the Christmas season for a full month—from December 6, *Svaty Mikuláš* Day (Saint Nicholas Day), to January 6, the Day of the Three Kings or Twelfth Night. Czech children are taught that Saint Nicholas descends from heaven on a golden rope and wanders the earth questioning children about their behavior and rewarding or punishing them as a result. He has two companions: an angel dressed in white carries a book to record the good or bad deeds of the children, while a devil called Cert, dressed in black, carries a whip and rattles a chain to remind the children who have been bad of what awaits them.

Until recently, there was a custom in Czech settlements in Texas associated with Saint Nicholas. Sometime between December 6 and Christmas Day a man wearing the white robes of a bishop and carrying a golden cross and a staff walked through the town rapping on doors and questioning the quaking children. Sometimes he was accompanied by the recording angel and the chain-rattling devil. Today Saint Nicholas comes after the children are asleep and fills stockings they have hung by the windows or by the foot of their beds. He judges the children in absentia, and those judged to have been naughty may find a stick or a potato or a piece of coal in their stockings. The judgment by Saint Nicholas is still used by parents to ensure good behavior, and it is not uncommon for them to rattle window blinds as a reminder to the children that Saint Nicholas may be watching them.

In some Czech families December 8, the Feast of the Immaculate Conception, is the day for good children to receive gifts of fruit and nuts placed in their shoes by Matíčka (the Blessed Mother) during the night. A Czech saying is that the weather on December 8 indicates what the weather will be on December 25. Long after the American Santa Claus (who evolved from Saint Nicholas) became the standard gift bringer on Christmas Eve, many Czech children continued also to receive gifts in stockings or shoes from Saint Nicholas or Matíčka on December 6 or 8.

In early Czech settlements in Texas it was customary for groups of carolers to go from house to house singing and being rewarded with treats of food and drink. The same hymns and carols are sung today by choral clubs who visit hospital patients, nursing home residents, and shut-ins. These Czech choral groups are on the increase. The Dallas Czech Singers are active, and the Seaton Choral Club, SPJST (Slavonic

Benevolent Order of the State of Texas) Lodge 47 regularly goes caroling to homes of shut-ins and gives concerts at nursing homes.

One of the most popular English carols is "Good King Wenceslas," written by an Englishman but about Saint Wenceslas (Václav) the martyred prince-duke of Bohemia in the tenth century, whose monumental statue dominates Wenceslas Square in Prague.

In the Czech carol "We are Going to the Stable" each shepherd on the way to see the newborn Christ Child plays an instrument: one a bagpipe, one a whistle, one a fiddle, and one a tuba. And the words imitate the sounds made by the instruments. The shepherds are apparently in a rollicking mood and declare they will "shout with glee and rock the cradle" when they find the baby.

Three of the most popular Czech carols are "Come, Hear the Wonderful Tidings," "Born Was Christ the Lord," and "The Rocking Carol":

> Jesus, Jesus, Baby dear, Baby dear
> We will rock Your cradle here.
> We will rock You, rock You, rock You,
> Gently slumber as we rock You,
> Jesus, Jesus do not fear,
> We who love You will be near.[3]

Today Czechs sing carols in English, but many still like to sing the enduring favorite "Silent Night," an Austrian carol that begins in Czech, "*Tichá Noc, Svatá Noc.*"

Weeks before Christmas, busy Czech cooks fill their homes with mouth-watering aromas as they bake their traditional Christmas breads, candies, cakes, and cookies. Given "Czech" in a word association test, most Texans might respond "kolache." Whether spelled *kolač, kolach, kolače, kolačky* or the anglicized kolache, these little sweet rolls are famous and popular the year round. During the Christmas season, they are given as treats and are served at social gatherings and with meals. They come with a variety of toppings. Fruit fillings were made from whatever kind of fruit grew in a certain area or was readily available. Texas Czechs might use pears or peaches; since cabbage and sauerkraut are such basic foods for Czechs, there is even a filling made of blanched cabbage mixed with coconut and sugar. Kolaches disappear so fast that they are usually made in large batches.[4]

Basic Kolache

1 stick butter, melted
2 cups warm milk
2 packages dry yeast
½ cup warm water
2 t. sugar

2 eggs
½ cup sugar
2 t. salt
8–9 cups flour

Combine butter and milk in a saucepan. Mix yeast, warm water, and 2 teaspoons sugar in large mixing bowl. Beat eggs in a cup with a fork, and add to butter and milk mixture. Combine this with yeast mixture. Add ½ cup sugar and salt. Gradually add sifted flour (8½ cups is usually sufficient) to make a stiff dough. Let mixture sit 15 minutes. Mix again until smooth. Let rise 50 minutes at 80°–85° or until double in bulk. After dough has risen, divide into egg-size portions with a spoon, and form into balls. Place on oiled baking sheet about 1 inch apart. Brush with melted butter. Let rise until light, then make an indentation in each ball. Fill with fruit filling and top with *posípka*. Makes 6 dozen.

FILLINGS

Prune
1 lb. prunes, cooked and pureed
1½ cups sugar

3 T. butter, melted
1 t. vanilla or cinnamon

Combine ingredients, and mix well.

Apricot
1 lb. dry apricots, cooked and
    pureed

3 T. butter, melted
½ t. almond flavoring

Combine ingredients, and mix well.

Cheese
1 lb. cottage cheese
1 cup sugar
pinch of salt

½ t. lemon rind
3 T. butter, melted
½ cup raisins (optional)

Combine ingredients, and mix well.

Poppy Seed
2 cups ground poppy seeds
1 cup milk
1½ cups sugar

2 T. flour
1 t. vanilla or almond flavoring

Heat milk in skillet to boiling. Add sugar, flour, and poppy seeds, and cook until thickened. Add flavoring.

Basic Kolache (cont.)

POSÍPKA (CRUMB TOPPING)

1 cup sugar   ½ cup flour
2 T. butter

Combine ingredients, and mix until like coarse meal.

Put fruit filling in indentations in balls of kolache dough. Sprinkle *posípka* over fruit filling. Let kolache dough rise again, about 20 minutes or until light to the touch. Bake at 450° for 15 minutes. Remove from oven. Again butter each kolache before removing from pan onto wire cooling rack or large board.

Czechs like spicy cookies, and the cookie with the most illustrious history is the *Pernik Na Figurky,* or gingerbread cookie, made into figures or shapes. In the Middle Ages these cookies were used to decorate tables and walls. At that time gingerbread was considered suitable only for the upper classes. As its use spread to the lower classes, bakers guarded their secret recipes that included a special mixture of spices, mainly ginger, which was imported at great expense. In the city of Prague alone there were as many as eighteen bakers in 1419. Their gingerbread cutters were of beautifully carved wood in shapes suitable for each festival or holiday. Today these molds, some of which were brought to Texas, are highly prized folk art objects. A popular Czech recipe for *pernicky* comes from Esther Bray.

For Christmas, gingerbread cookies are often decorated with an icing made of powdered sugar and egg whites, which may have food colors added, and with almonds. The imagination of the gingerbread artist is the only limitation on the range of shapes and decoration of the cookies. They appear as angels, stars, and hearts. Many cookies are shaped like animals, including birds and especially fish, with which the Czechs have a fascination.

Christmas Eve is a day of fasting for those who observe church ritual. Czech children are still told that if they do not eat until evening they will see the "golden pig." But no one is able to describe the pig. All of the adults interviewed admitted that they had never managed to

Gingerbread Men
Esther L. Bray

1 cup soft butter	1 t. soda
½ cup granulated sugar	2 t. salt
½ cup packed light brown sugar	1 t. ginger
⅓ cup molasses	1 t. cinnamon
⅔ cup light corn syrup	½ t. cloves
4½ cups flour	raisins or currants

Cream butter and sugars together until light. Add molasses and corn syrup, and mix well. Add sifted dry ingredients, kneading dough until smooth. Chill several hours or until firm enough to roll. Roll out on lightly floured board to ⅛-inch thickness. Cut out with cookie cutter, and place on lightly greased baking sheet. Place raisins or currants on cookies for facial features and coat buttons. Bake at 350° for about 8 minutes or until lightly browned. Cool on racks. Store in airtight container. Makes about 3 dozen.

make it without food on the fasting day with all the tantalizing aromas of Christmas baking filling the house.

Christmas Eve supper is a festive meal. Often money is placed under each plate to ensure prosperity. In Czechoslovakia carp is the main dish.[6] The carp may be bought alive and kept in the family bathtub. In Texas, some Czech families still have fish as the entree on Christmas Eve, but it is catfish, oysters, shrimp, or some other kind of local fish. Lentils, peas, potatoes, barley soup with mushrooms, and apple strudel are usually included in the meal. A special Christmas bread is traditionally served at supper, but since it resembles a coffee cake, modern Czech families frequently serve it for breakfast. This "bread" is called *vánočka* – the Czech word for Christmas is *Vánoce*.

Not finding their beloved fir trees in the sections of Texas where they settled, the Czech immigrants adopted the abundant cedar tree as a substitute. Usually the grown-ups and older children of a family decorated the tree on the afternoon of December 24, and it was kept behind locked doors until after the evening meal. After someone had slipped away from the table and lighted the candles, a bell rang and the small children raced to see the tree for the first time in all its shining beauty. Many Czechs have preserved or returned to traditional ways of

Best Christmas Wishes

CHRISTMAS GREETING

May the love of the
worshiping shepherds
Abound in your heart to-day

May the spirit of·
the Christmastide
remain with you
throughout the year··

Also hat Gott die Welt geliebt, daß Er Seinen
eingeborenen Sohn gab. Joh. 3, 16.

Gesegnete Weihnachten!

May Good Luck follow where'er you go,
Like Mary's little lamb, you know

May these wishes bring you blessings
Of such perfect joy and cheer,
That you will know all gladness
Through each day of this New Year

Christmas Bread (Vánočka)

2 yeast cakes	2 egg yolks
1 cup milk	5 cups flour
2 t. sugar	½ cup raisins
1 stick butter	½ cup blanched almonds, chopped
½ cup sugar	1 egg, beaten
½ t. salt	1 T. milk
2 eggs	

Crumble yeast into 1 cup lukewarm milk (if dry yeast is used, dissolve in a small amount of milk first). Add 2 teaspoons sugar, and let rise. Cream butter, sugar, salt, 2 eggs, and the 2 additional egg yolks. Add half the flour, and mix well. Add yeast, and mix in remainder of flour. Mix well, then turn out on floured board, and knead thoroughly until dough is smooth. Place in a bowl, and cover. Let rise in a warm place about 1½ hours or until double in bulk. Turn out on floured board again, and knead, adding raisins and almonds. Divide dough into 6 even parts. Roll each piece into 15-inch rope. Place 3 ropes on well-greased baking sheet, sealing together at one end. Braid ropes and seal the other end. Twist together 2 of the remaining ropes and place on top of braid. Finally, twist the remaining rope and place on the top. Let rise again for about 1 hour. Brush dough lightly with mixture of beaten egg and 1 tablespoon milk. Bake at 350° for 45 minutes.[7]

decorating their trees. This means using natural objects, such as fruit and nuts, handmade decorations, and homemade foods. Bright red apples, cookies, walnuts wrapped in shiny foil, multicolored paper chains, popcorn strings, and candles made of beeswax are also used. Candies wrapped in foil hang from the tree limbs along with the decorated cookies. A Bethlehem or manger scene may be found under the tree, as might a loaf of sweet bread in the shape of a lamb.

In pre–Santa Claus days, Czech children believed that the gifts under the tree were from the Christ Child. Today most go along with the idea that Santa Claus or Saint Nicholas (the two are often fused and the names used interchangeably) brings the gifts. After the gifts are distributed, the family might sing carols and play games. Some of these games are very ancient ones that attempt to look into the future. They are often of the good luck–bad luck variety or are connected with wedding predictions.

One popular game is to place tiny candles in walnut-shell boats and float them in a pan of water. The player whose candle goes out last will have the best luck. But those whose candles flicker or go out quickly can expect misfortune. Likewise if the shell capsizes, danger is near. Sometimes a candle is placed by each person's supper plate, and the one whose candle goes out first is expected to be the first to die.[8]

Several popular fortune-telling games use apples and nuts. In one, each girl peels an apple, keeping the peel intact. Then she throws it over the heads of the other girls. Whatever letter the peel seems to form after it lands is the first initial of the boy she will marry.

In another game, each player cuts an apple in half horizontally. The position of the seeds predicts the future for that person. If the seeds form a star, all is well. If they are in a circle, life will continue, but if a cross is formed, illness or death will come within the next year. Another prognosticating game involves giving seven nuts to each person. The players are allowed to select and crack three of their nuts, and the player who cracks the plumpest nut will receive seven years of good luck.

Many Czechs are familiar with a Christmas foretelling game in which lead is melted in an old spoon and poured into cold water. If an unmarried girl is the player, the shape the lead takes reveals the occupation of her future husband. (The game obviously requires a good imagination.) In another version, players glimpse the future by interpreting the shadow made when the lead is held next to a wall. A ship forecasts a voyage; a gun or other weapon means the player will become a soldier; a flower predicts happiness; and a cross means illness or death lurks nearby.

An old Czech belief is that shooting a gun on Christmas Eve drives off evil spirits, and the early Texas Czech settlers acted accordingly. Today their descendants carry on the tradition, if not the belief, by shooting off fireworks, whereas their grandparents might have used dynamite or anvils packed with gunpowder.

Many Czech families, especially Catholics, go to midnight church services on Christmas Eve. The churches usually feature nativity scenes, sometimes with live actors. The singing of favorite hymns and carols is an important part of these services. Christmas Day for Czech fami-

A hearty wish, a fervent hope
That Christmastide
may bring to you and yours,
Good cheer, good health,
good luck in everything.

lies is usually a family day featuring a feast that typically includes soup, chicken or turkey, dumplings, kolaches, fruit, and nuts. Prunes are a favorite food, and often they are mixed with raisins as well as being used as kolache toppings. Prune dumplings or butterhorns filled with prunes may appear on the Christmas menu. In earlier days roast goose or duck, raised on the family farm and stuffed with a sauerkraut dressing flavored with caraway seeds, was usually the main course. But today a turkey frequently replaces the traditional goose, and sauerkraut is served as a side dish. Besides coffee and tea, early Czech pioneers served wine made from mustang grapes, honey wine (mead) made from their own honey, and homemade beer. Coffee, tea, and beer are still favored drinks.

In Europe, Saint Stephen's Day (December 26) was a time when farm hands moved on to new jobs and were given generous parting gifts. The Czech version of an eastern European saying is that "on St. Stephen's Day there is no master." Although the custom is no longer even remembered by many Czechs, they still sing a holiday gift song connected with customs of that time long ago:

Sing, sing Stephen
What do you carry in the jug?
I am carrying my gifts,
But I have fallen on the ice
And the dogs have jumped on me,
And they ate all my gifts.
But don't laugh at me!
They gave me their gifts
But still they laugh at me![9]

Today Saint Stephen's Day is a time for Texas Czechs to relax, visit with family, eat the leftover Christmas goodies, and play card games. Some of these games involve Tarot cards. Many Czech families have Tarot cards imported from Czechoslovakia that are like beautiful works of art, and they are treasured for their beauty and design. *Taroky,* a game using these cards and involving four players, is popular among young and old.

Czechs usher in the new year with gusto. Dances are the order of the day or evening on December 31. Every fraternal group has a New Year's Eve dance. The Czech word for a social gathering is *beseda,* which is also the name of the national dance of Czechoslovakia. Polkas and waltzes are favored dances, and the catchy rhythms of the polka bands make it almost impossible for spectators not to sing or sway or at least pat their feet in time to the music. Popular with Texas audiences are "Red Wine and White Kolache Polka," "Roll Out the Barrel Polka," "Grinder's Polka," "Looking for My Sweetheart Waltz," and "Happiness Waltz." Earlier bands were often composed only of brass instruments, or they might feature a dulcimer or piano. Today they range from brass bands to orchestras. Button or piano accordians are popular, as are electric steel guitars.

Dance groups in Texas wear the Czech native folk costume or *kroje* at performances. These colorful costumes were brought to Texas by early settlers and later reproduced here. The basic costume for the woman consists of a full red skirt embroidered with flowers and a white blouse with big, puffed sleeves. The shawl is embroidered in black and edged with black lace, while the closely fitted vest is red and trimmed with beads. The embroidered black apron has beige lace at the bottom. Married women wear beaded and embroidered caps while unmarried women wear a half wreath of flowers in their hair. Boots and black stockings complete the outfit. Different groups may vary the colors of this basic

costume. The man's costume consists of fitted braid-trimmed pants with a full-sleeved, embroidered, lace-trimmed blouse and a colored vest decorated with ribbons. In Texas both men and women often substitute black shoes for boots.

New Year's is another time for trying to peer into the future, and again various means of prophecy are used. An old custom for foretelling the health of the family is to have each family member crack twelve nuts, representing the months of the coming year. A bad nut indicates illness. Thus if a person's fourth nut is bad, illness can be expected in April. A Czech superstition is that the ear or jowl of a hog must be eaten on January 1 to ensure happiness and prosperity in the coming year. But nowadays Texas Czechs prefer to serve more appealing portions of the pig, such as pork loin roasts, for their New Year's Day feast. Sauerkraut or some form of cabbage is a usual accompaniment.

Since the majority of the Czechs who came to Texas had farms, the weather played an important role in determining their fortunes. They, in turn, tried to determine what the weather would be like during the coming year. Two variations of weather forecasting were popular. The twelve days from Christmas to January 6 or the first twelve days of the new year might be used. In either case, the weather during these twelve days was supposed to be comparable to the weather during the corresponding month. Probably the outcome is as reliable as any other means of forecasting Texas weather.

The Day of the Three Wise Men, January 6, is observed in Czechoslovakia by the ritual of having groups of boys dressed in long white robes and wearing paper crowns visit homes. With chalk that has been blessed by a priest, they write on the lintels above the doors the initials of the Three Kings: Kaspar, Melchior, and Balthazar—K+M+B—and the year. Then they sing songs in honor of the Wise Men, whom they represent. The families in the homes they visit reward them with money or small gifts of food for the good fortune they have supposedly bestowed by their visit. This custom was carried to Texas, and today it is still observed through the marking of the entrance doorways of churches with "K+M+B" and the year. And there are individual families in Granger and other places who use blessed chalk to mark the initials over the entranceways to their homes in remembrance of the Three Wise Men who visited the Christ Child.

Traditionally, Czechs take down their trees on January 6. By this time their thoughts are already turning to their next great holiday. Soon it will be time to plan Easter services, to prepare special food for this celebration, and to decorate the gorgeous Easter eggs for which they are famous.

Barnfests and Lutefisk:

THE SCANDINAVIAN HERITAGE

Glaedelig Jul! Descendants of Vikings—Danes, Norwegians, and Swedes—have brought interesting Christmas legends to Texas. One of these is about Santa Lucia, a martyr who lived in Syracuse in the fourth century. She was said to have brought food to her fellow Christians in the catacombs, wearing candles on her head to keep her hands free. Supposedly she also appeared during a famine in Sweden (many years after her death), surrounded by a halo of light and distributing food to the people. Santa Lucia Day, December 13, begins the Christmas season for Swedish people. In private homes a young girl of the family traditionally dresses as Santa Lucia in a white robe with a red sash and a crown of greenery studded with candles. She awakens her parents by bringing them a tray with sweet buns, called Lucia buns, and coffee. In Sweden public pageants mark the day, and recently Texas organizations have sponsored Swedish programs featuring young women playing the role of Santa Lucia.

The first Swede known to immigrate to Texas was Swen (or Svante) Magnus Swenson, a remarkable man of legendary reputation. He had the Midas touch in business, establishing successful operations in the mercantile business as well as in banking, hotel operation, land, and cotton. He is probably best known today as the founder of the extensive SMS ranches, still operated by his descendants. Swenson is also remembered for bringing from his homeland tales of a gift giver who traveled in a magic reindeer-drawn sleigh. For over twenty years Swenson worked to recruit other Swedish immigrants. His chief recruit was his uncle, Svante Palm, who became known as another Renaissance man in Texas.

The majority of Scandinavian immigrants arrived in Texas in the late nineteenth century, and place names reveal their heritage: Norse in Bosque County, New Sweden in Travis County, and Danevang (Danish meadow) in Wharton County. In their communities the Texas Norsemen formed mutual assistance societies and continued their ancient customs, especially those connected with holidays.

The term *yule* comes from the Norse and Anglo-Saxons, who in pagan times burned a huge oak log called the *juul* (pronounced yool) to honor Thor, the god of thunder. After the Norse became Christians, they made the Yule log an important part of their Christmas ceremonies. Probably Swen Swenson was inspired to retell his old Christmas tales to his Texas friends as they sat around a Yule log on his plantation.

For many Scandinavians the most memorable figure connected with Christmas is Jule-Nissen, a little old elf who lives in the attic or hayloft and is seen only by the family cat. Like the American gremlin, he is responsible for odd or mischievous happenings that no one else will admit to having caused. But he is also helpful, and takes care of the animals if they are neglected. On Christmas Eve the children of the family put out a bowl of rice porridge for him. Next morning when they rush to examine the bowl, it is always empty. Modern Texans of Scandinavian heritage use little *jule-nissen* figures as decorations. Sometimes the little elf, dressed in gray with a red pointed cap and long white whiskers, dances in his clogs as a mobile hung from the ceiling. There is a Swedish ghost, a *tomte,* who is also a dwarf. He likes to sit in a corner and watch the family Christmas fun. If food is placed for him where no one can observe it, he will eat it and leave. The Norwegians use brooms to sweep out ghosts; they call it sweeping out Christmas.

Straw was once important in Scandinavian Christmas observances, as it was thought to have magical qualities. Today, Scandinavians like to display decorations such as straw stars and straw billy goats, once sinister but now benign guardians of the Christmas tree.

A lovely tradition in Scandinavian countries is to give special treats to animals and birds at Christmas time. Generous helpings of the best grain are given to horses and cows. In earlier times in Norway the cattle were given a good portion of the Yule ale. The birds had their own Christmas trees, made from sheaves of unthreshed grain, saved from the harvest and tied to poles. In remembrance of this custom, some Norse Texans tie sheaves of grain to sticks or over doorposts for the birds.

Weeks of food preparation precede Christmas Eve, when the Norse enjoy a big dinner. A custom still practiced in Texas is for the father of a family to leave the house after dinner and return as Santa Claus. A more startling custom is for the Swedish family to receive gifts by having them tossed in through a (deliberately left open) door or window. A neighbor or friend is engaged to throw the presents, which are appropriately labeled with the name of the intended recipient.

For the predominantly Protestant Norse, the important religious service has been in the early morning on Christmas Day. This early service (*Julatta* in Swedish) at five or six A.M. memorializes the early morning visit of the shepherds to the manger. However, many Norse now follow the custom of holding services on Christmas Eve at four or five P.M., since it was at this time that the village church bells chimed in the old country signaling the beginning of the Christmas rituals. In a beautifully preserved rock church built in 1886 between Cranfills Gap and Norse, candlelight Christmas Eve services are held. The candles give a special quality to the service, and they are necessary since the church has no electricity.

Scandinavians like to decorate their Christmas trees with strings of small flags, which are colorful replicas of their national flags. Hearts made of different materials and small woven baskets filled with candy are also popular ornaments. Norwegian children are told that spiders crawled on the Christmas tree and spun the glistening decorations during the night.

A Danish custom is for everyone to form a ring around the Christmas tree and dance, skip, or glide while singing carols. In Danevang this tradition has been observed in homes and at the community center since the town was founded in 1894. Young and old join hands and form four circles, with the youngest children in the innermost circle. They dance around a cedar decorated with old-fashioned ornaments and sing American and Danish carols. "Nu Är Det Jul Igen" ("Now We Have Christmas Again"), a lively carol, is a favorite. The three verses "Now we have Christmas again; Now we have Christmas again; Christmas lasts until Easter" are sung over and over, faster and faster, as the circles go first one way and then the other. The dancing is followed by refreshments and visiting.

A traditional *Barnfest,* or children's program, held the day after Christmas has always been a highlight of the season for the settlement at New Sweden. Weeks of preparation include having the children memorize speeches and songs. Parents and grandparents fill the church to capacity on this festive night. In later years the program date became moveable, and used projectors and screens, but the Christmas tree continues to hold gifts of books, candy, and fruit for the children and an apple for each adult.

"Shooting in Christmas," a custom practiced by Norwegian settlers, supposedly began in ancient times because of the belief that witches roamed the countryside on Christmas Eve. Young men crept up outside houses and shot their guns to frighten off the evil spirits and, no doubt, to frighten the inhabitants out of their wits. This custom suited pioneer Texans, who had a tendency to celebrate the season noisily. A quieter way of avoiding ill luck in all the Scandinavian countries was to let the Yule candle burn throughout the night until the sun rose, and then to use the remainder of the candle to make the sign of the cross on the cattle.

Mistletoe becomes big business each December in Central Texas. Exactly how mistletoe became connected with Christmas is unknown. It was sacred to the Druids, and early Teutons used it for decoration. The Norse believed that mistletoe in the house protected the house from loss by fire. And Swedes placed mistletoe in stalls to keep witches from riding or injuring their horses. Today Texas Scandinavians use mistletoe in the same way other Europeans, Americans, and Canadians do—as a charming decoration with romantic overtones.

Christmas seals are a unique Danish contribution to the season. They originated in Denmark in 1903 to raise funds to build a hospital for children suffering from tuberculosis. Four years later the first seals were sold in America.

Hans Christian Andersen, Denmark's beloved writer of fairy tales, wrote a poem that became the text for one of the Danes' best-known carols. Out of his own bittersweet experience, Andersen wrote the inspiring words to "Barn (Child) Jesus":

Child Jesus

Child Jesus came to earth this day,
To save us sinners dying

And cradled in the straw and hay
The Holy One is lying.
The star shines down the child to greet,
The lowing oxen kiss his feet.
Hallelujah, Hallelujah, Child Jesus!

Take courage, Soul so weak and worn,
Thy sorrows have departed.
A Child in David's town is born,
To heal the broken hearted.
Then let us haste this child to find
And children be in heart and mind.
Hallelujah, Hallelujah, Child Jesus![1]

Rice porridge or pudding, made with milk, sprinkled with cinnamon and sugar, and baked with an almond hidden in it is a must for many Scandinavian families on Christmas Eve. It was served as a first course in Denmark, and whoever found the almond had to keep it a secret until all the porridge was eaten; otherwise the suspense would have been over and the unexciting dish left unfinished. A prize was given to the finder of the almond. Today some Danish families serve rice desserts with a hidden almond just for the fun of it, and the person finding the almond receives a small box of candy or some other trifling gift.

On Christmas Day the Danes usually had an entree of goose stuffed with prunes or a pork roast served with sour cabbage. For dessert the famous Danish apple cake, still very popular in Texas, was common.

Aeblekage (Danish Apple Cake)

2 cups toasted bread crumbs	2½ cups applesauce containing
1 T. sugar	pieces of fresh apples
½ t. cinnamon	½ pt. whipping cream
¼ cup butter	2 T. sugar

Crumbs may be from dried French bread, toasted white bread, zwieback, cake, or a combination of these. Brown crumbs in a skillet with 1 tablespoon sugar, cinnamon, and butter. Place prepared crumbs in well-buttered 9 × 9 × 2-inch baking dish in layers alternating with cooked applesauce. Bake 1 hour at 350°. Unmold. Serve cold with a generous helping of whipped cream, sweetened with 2 tablespoons sugar. Decorate with dabs of red jelly.

Christmas would not be Christmas to the Danes without *pebber-nodder* (peppernuts), tiny, spicy cookies flavored with almonds and white pepper.

Pebbernodder
(Deluxe Peppernuts)

5 cups flour	1½ cups sugar
1½ cups butter	⅛ t. white pepper
1 t. vanilla	½ cup finely chopped almonds

Mix all ingredients together. Form into rolls ½ inch in diameter. Cut into small pieces, and drop on buttered baking sheets. Bake at 350° for 12–15 minutes. The cookies may be rolled in colored sugars before baking. Store in tightly closed tins. Makes about 8 dozen.

Norwegian settlers in Bosque County ate lutefisk (codfish steeped in lye) on Christmas Eve—if they could get it. Today they make sure to have it by importing it in hundred-bale lots.[2] Much of the lutefisk is consumed at the annual Lutefisk Festival in Cranfills Gap. The fish arrives from the fjords of Norway in pieces up to three feet long. Its dehydrated form is so hard that it takes a saw to cut through it. It is patiently rejuvenated by repeated soakings: in lye water for three or four days, changing the water daily; in lime water for three or four days, stirring often and changing the water daily; and finally in clear water, changing the water twice a day. The lutefisk comes out about five times as large as in its dried form; 250 pounds of dried fish converts to fifteen hundred pounds of edible fish. The final step is to boil the fish for about three minutes while watching it carefully—a minute too long and it becomes an inedible mush.

The Lutefisk Festival, which is held at the school cafeteria in Cranfills Gap in December, attracts close to a thousand people annually to the small community. It began as a fund-raising project, sponsored by Saint Olaf's Lutheran Church, for the local school. When it got too big for the church to handle, it was taken over by the Cranfills Gap Booster Club. It takes the whole community to make it work. In addition to preparing the fish and arranging the dining area, local people—Norwegians and otherwise—donate the white sauce, potatoes, green beans, cranberries, homemade bread, and pies that round out the meal, plus the turkey and dressing served to those who have not yet learned to love lutefisk. High school girls in Norwegian costumes serve the dinner. Visitors waiting their turns at the long tables are entertained by Norwegian folk dancing teams. A satisfied diner described the ritual of eating the meal: "First the steaming lutefisk is put on the plate. On top of this goes a generous serving of boiled white potatoes. Next comes melted butter—and plenty of it. Then comes a white sauce. These four layers are then mashed and eaten . . . delicious!"[3]

During the holidays, Scandinavian Texans like to entertain in their homes with a *julebord* or Christmas table which, like a smorgasbord, means a tableful of tempting food. The festively decorated buffet table may be covered with two dozen different dishes. Featured are sure to be seafoods including *sursild* (sour herring with onion, pepper, and dills), herring salad with chopped apple, potato, beets, and onion, and shrimp salad. *Rodkal* (sweet and sour red cabbage), miniature meat patties, cheese, fruit, and crackers can also be found. Cold aquavit, which is a Scandinavian liqueur, and beer are offered. For the finale there is coffee and a selection of traditional cookies such as *sandnotter* and *sandbakkels*.

Sandbakkels
Mrs. Loyd S. Swenson

1 cup butter, softened	1 egg
1 cup shortening	4–4½ cups all-purpose flour
2 cups sugar	

Combine butter, shortening, and sugar. Cream until light and fluffy. Beat in egg. Gradually add flour, and continue beating to form dough. Keep adding flour until dough no longer sticks to fingers when handled.

Place dough into individual sandbakkel forms or patty shells, making sure no dough extends over edges of molds. Place forms on cookie sheet, and bake at 350° for 5 minutes. Remove from molds, and cool completely. Store in airtight containers. Makes about 7 dozen.

Sandbakkels, crisp butter cookies, baked in fluted molds or tiny foil cups, are a favorite Norwegian treat to serve to carolers or guests.

British and Anglo-American settlers brought the idea of the wassail bowl to Texas, but originally it had been imported to England from Scandinavia by Henry VII. The term *wassail* comes from Old Norse *ves heill* meaning "be well" or "be hale." Texas Scandinavians gathered around wassail bowls might give the proper response, which is drink "hael" or drink well–unnecessary advice for any good Viking.

Le Père Noël:

THE FRENCH HERITAGE

Joyeux Noël! One Frenchman, living in Texas while it was still a Spanish province, celebrated the Christmas season with profane enthusiasm. For Jean Lafitte,[1] with his band of smugglers and privateers, the Christmas–New Year's season was a time for drunken carousing in the group's Galveston headquarters. These buccaneers specialized in concocting a potent punch out of rum and sugar pirated from merchant ships sailing the Gulf of Mexico. Texan historian J. O. Dyer described the brew: "The rum was stronger, the hot water more muddled, and the sugar was damp, brown, and molasses-flavored, and in the buccaneer camps they got both spices and limes from Jamaica, and when the condiments were lacking a little red pepper took the place and added 'kick' to the taste. . . ."[2]

The rum ration was tripled in the pirate camp on holidays, and on New Year's Day rude practical jokes and horseplay accompanied the heavy drinking. One recorded New Year's Day prank was to urge a newcomer or landlubber to turn over a stinging Portuguese man-of-war to find out how many pearls were growing in its stomach.

Some of the privateers who could write sharpened their quill pens and their wits to write crude rhymes ridiculing their companions. These squibs, sometimes written using blood as ink, satirized physical weaknesses and personality defects—much like our more recent comic Valentine's cards. A jumbled patois of French, English, Portuguese, and Spanish prevailed in the Galveston camp. One of the surviving New Year's lampoons, with its translation, reads:

> En voila jo ami le boeuf,
> Il ne Jamais argent eneuf,

Et quand desiro demand l'oeuf,
Tout suite esta dumb and deaf.[3]

Here comes your friendly ox,
Never has money enough,
And when you wish to ask an egg (slang for loan)
He at once is dumb and deaf.

French contributions to Texas history have been both romantic and humorous. They gave us the Pastry War and the Pig War. But it was a dashing young dreamer named René Robert Cavelier, Sieur de La Salle who gave France its claim to Texas in the seventeenth century by establishing Fort Saint Louis on its soil. His murder in Texas by his own men adds poignancy to the drama of his adventurous life.

Today two main enclaves of French descendants live in Texas. One group lives in and around picturesque Castroville, where French empresario Henri Castro settled his colony of Alsatians in the 1840s. The other concentration of Texans of French extraction resides in the Beaumont–Port Arthur–Orange triangle, where French Cajuns spilled over the Texas-Louisiana border. In several Texas cities a club, L'Alliance Française, helps perpetuate the French language, customs, and traditions.

In 1839, the ambitious Alphonse de Saligny was appointed France's chargé d'affaires to the Republic of Texas. Saligny, who loved his creature comforts, was a misfit in the tiny, raw frontier village of Austin. He brought with him his butler, his Parisian-trained cook, and his other servants, and he put on entertainments to impress the pioneer Texans. During the holiday season of 1840 he gave lavish dinner parties in his rented quarters, to which he invited Sam Houston and members of the Texas legislature. Congressman Isaac Van Zandt described one of these dinners in a letter to his wife: "It was the most brilliant affair I ever saw, the most massive plate of silver and gold, the finest glass, and everything exceeded anything I ever saw. We sat at the table four hours— I was wearied to death but had to stand it with the company. We had plates changed about fifteen times."[4]

Count de Saligny (as he liked to style himself) built and furnished the so-called French Embassy in Austin. Today Texans know the well-preserved building as the French Legation, a treasured reminder of Texas' days as a republic. In December each year the French Legation Committee of the Daughters of the Republic of Texas holds a holiday open house and gift bazaar to raise funds for the maintenance of the historic building. Visitors sample nineteenth-century refreshments and take a tour of the rooms, which are decorated in nineteenth-century style. Wreathed with greenery, a portrait of King Louis Philippe watches haughtily over the activities.

Another colorful, early Frenchman in Texas was Henri Domenech, a Roman Catholic abbé, who found himself in Castroville in the winter of 1847. Wishing to decorate the temporary church in honor of the season, he traveled by horseback to San Antonio to obtain some cloths. Returning to Castroville after dark, he found the road slippery and dangerous as a sleety rain began to fall. Soon his cloak stiffened under a layer of ice. His hands too stiff to hold the bridle, he had to let his horse take its own way. As they approached Castroville, wolves began to howl nearby. Pursued by the wolves, the terrified horse sped home with the abbé. No sooner had the exhausted priest settled down in his bed than he was roused by a choir of young men singing German Christmas hymns to compliment him, for his birthday was on the twenty-fifth of December. Soon many other colonists arrived with cakes and pork to congratulate him.

The next day the abbé, as a surprise for his congregation, secretly lighted a flame of Bengal fire,[5] concealed behind flowers. But the surprise turned out to be on him:

> I had on a vestment of cloth of gold, and at the moment when I gave out the Te Deum the flame suddenly illuminated the church like an Aurora Borealis; the gold, the crystals, the chandeliers, seemed electrified; the sacred hymn was chaunted with redoubled zeal and energy; but the proverb says, "there's no fire without smoke," and that had not entered into my calculation. With the flame rose clouds of smoke, which soon nearly suffocated us, and the whole congregation coughed in a frightful manner for nearly five minutes; fortunately our church had openings in all directions and the smoke cleared off. . . .[6]

In 1852 the indomitable Abbé Domenech was stationed in Brownsville where he conducted an ecumenical Christmas service with a sensuous mixture of religious and secular elements:

> Christmas-day arrived, with its rejoicings for the people. During the midnight mass, I had a moment's happiness in seeing a crowd of every age, sex, and creed, take possession of the house of God, which was

at this moment in all its splendour. The draperies, the flowers, the lights, supplied in profusion, were in sweet harmony with the French taste, become proverbial with strangers.

The mass was sung by fourteen of my countrymen who had very sweet voices. The chasuble which I wore, was the gift of a Mexican. It was gold brocade embroidered with gold and silk; and though more than a hundred years old, it reflected rays of light in all directions. Upwards of 300 who could find no room in the church had to hear mass in the open air. Fireworks, sent off by the officers of the garrison, terminated this feast, which had never before been celebrated with so much solemnity on the frontiers of Texas.[7]

The French missionary spent an exhausting week. He had no assistants to help him as he heard Christmas confessions, decorated the church, explained the ceremonies in two languages, and sang by himself all the entire offices, which were very long.

Although stories differ about the origin of the Christmas tree, most writers agree that the first trees of record were at Strasbourg in Alsace, France. The record is negative in tone. A 1561 Alsatian ordinance tried to limit the size of the trees by forbidding the cutting of bushes "more than the length of eight shoes" for Christmas use. Originally the trees decorated with fruit and holy wafers hung upside down from the rafters. By the mid-sixteenth century the trees stood upright with secular decorations including tinsel and candles, and the holy wafers had become cookies. The church did not approve. In 1740, a minister in Strasbourg complained: "Among other trifles with which the people often occupy the Christmas time is the Christmas tree, which they erect in the house, hang with dolls and sugar and cause to lose its bloom. Where the habit comes from I do not know. Far better that children be dedicated to the spiritual cedar tree, Jesus Christ."[8]

The French, however, did not give up their trees, and for many years in the Alsatian villages in Texas the trees were given more importance than the gifts, which were typically fruit, nuts, sweets, and a small toy or two. Women took great pains with the cookies used to decorate the trees, creating a wide variety of shapes with tin cookie cutters or homemade cardboard patterns. They designed all sorts of animals, birds, stars, and hearts as well as angels and human figures. They decorated them with silver dragées, colored sugar, and tiny candy beads before hanging them by strings on the trees. Homemade candy was wrapped in colored tissue paper with fringed ends and tied to the branches or placed in tiny baskets. The edible decorations included oranges and apples, rare treats seen only at Christmastime.

Paper ornaments constructed out of glossy pictures framed with tinsel had both secular and religious symbols: for example, an angel riding a fish next to Santa with his bag of toys. Candles in little holders that clipped onto the branches made the silver dragées glisten and heightened the mingled odor of oranges and cedar. The Cajuns in East Texas today decorate trees with pinecones, holly, popcorn strings, handmade paper chains, and small white crocheted doilies resembling snowflakes.

The French gave us the word *crèche* for the Nativity scene. In their cathedrals and in their homes the French made *crèches* a focus of worship at Christmas. Traditionally, Christmas Eve combines social and religious functions for French families. They may invite a few intimate friends to drink wine or eggnog to while away the hours before attending *la messe de minuit* (midnight mass). After mass there is a joyous *reveillon* or midnight breakfast. In East Texas is has a distinctly Cajun flavor and will likely include eggs in different styles, sweet breads, jellied meat, raisin bread, crisp French bread, cakes or molded desserts topped with mountains of whipped cream, and several different wines. In Castroville where the customs of other ethnic groups have intertwined with those of the French settlers, holiday meals include sausage dishes, tamales, potato pancakes, and mustang grape wine.

Until recently, Christmas Day for French Texans remained a quiet day of family religious observances, and New Year's Day was the time for gift giving and visiting. The French Santa, le Père Noël, evolved over the years, like all the other Santas, from Saint Nicholas. Originally, le Père Fouettard, "the whipping father," accompanied le Père Noël when he visited children and asked about their behavior. Le Père Fouettard was a weasel-faced old man with a long gray beard and threatening dark eyes. He carried a wicker basket filled with switches that he left for naughty children. Originally Père Noël traveled on a donkey carrying his presents in a basket on his back. In each home he found a row of small shoes by the hearth, each shoe holding a few coins for him and a carrot for his donkey. For modern children of French descent, Père Noël has merged with the ubiquitous American Santa Claus.

The german was a French dance performed in a circle and consisting of intricate figures directed by a floor manager. Though it was out of vogue in France, it gained great popularity in nineteenth-century Texas. In the Castroville area, holiday dances included a mixture of Anglo-American, German, and French elements. Old-timers still remember the popularity of "Herr Schmitt," a German folk dance, and the American "Sweet Bunch of Daisies" as well as their old French tunes. Fiddles, or later pianos, furnished the music for dancing polkas, one-steps, two-steps, seven-steps, schottisches, flea hops, "Put Your Little Foot," and above all the waltz, performed with exuberant hopping and twirling. Cajuns in East Texas have always loved dancing, especially lively two-steps, but today they jitterbug to the music. A single accordian may furnish the music for an entire evening of dancing, called a *fais-dodo*, at the community dance hall, where dances are held frequently during the holidays.

The French have given to Texas and to the world some of the loveliest carols, including "Carol of the Birds" and "Carol of the Flowers." A French composer, Adolphe Charles Adam, wrote "O Holy Night," and an American minister, John Dwight, gave it its familiar words: "O holy night! The stars are brightly shining / It is the night of the dear savior's birth. . . ." "Angels o'er the Fields Were Singing," probably from the eighteenth century, is well-known for its ringing refrain: "Gloria in excelsis Deo" drawn out over seven measures. Another French carol, "Il Est Né, le Divin Enfant" ("He Is Born, the Holy Child") sounds so stirring in French that often the first line is sung in French even when the rest of the song is sung in English. Bernard de la Monnoye, an eighteenth-century composer, wrote many lively songs, including some ribald ones. His carol "Pat-a-Pan" exemplifies the ebullient attitude of the French toward most things in their lives, including their religion. The first stanza says:

> Willie, get your little drum
> Robin, bring your flute, and come.
> Aren't they fun to play upon?
> Turelurelu, patapatapan
> When you pay your fife and drum
> How can anyone be glum?

And the last stanza concludes:

God and man today become
Closely joined as flute and drum.
Let the joyous tune play on!
Turelurelu, patapatapan
As the instruments you play,
We will sing, this Christmas day![9]

The tune of "Jingle Bells" quickly caught the French fancy, but they have put their own words to it, and it has become "Vive le Vent," a song about the wind.

The French have a reputation for being able to turn the most ordinary meals into festive occasions. From onion soup to ambrosia, their way with food is legendary for its distinctive touches. Although the French Texans in the Castroville region recognized the excellence of some of their German neighbors' dishes, they couldn't resist giving them a French twist with a soupçon of this or that and a petit sauce. They made anise cookies but set them out to rise in the sun. Why? "Because they puff better," said with a shrug, is the only answer.

The French have characteristically treated their older people with respect bordering on reverence. There is a special relationship between French godparents and their godchildren. Traditionally, a godmother prepares a special New Year's bread on New Year's Eve, knowing her godchildren will stop by to pick up their individual loaves (which sometimes have their initials on them) to eat at breakfast on New Year's Day for good luck.

Parisa is a popular appetizer served at celebrations in the Castroville region. Each community has added its own distinctive touches. This version is featured at the Folklife Festival in San Antonio. A D'Hanis version of parisa calls for ten medium-sized green chili peppers, chopped.

Among the Cajuns of East Texas, dishes have their own Louisiana French flavor. Sweet potato pie, cracklin' bread, and gumbo made with chicken and homemade sausage are favorites.

The kitchen of the French Legation in Austin is a reconstruction of an early French Creole kitchen. On display in this kitchen at the "Christmas at the French Legation" open house is a *buche de Noël* (Christmas cake), which is a traditional chocolate cake rolled to look like a Yule log. A French Texan might serve this cake at a Christmas dinner to be

Alsatian New Year's Bread
Aunt Molly Hans Schott

1½ cups milk, scalded
½ cup butter
¾ cup sugar
2 pkgs. dry yeast
½ cup warm water
2 eggs, beaten

½ cup raisins (optional)
1 sifter-full flour (5 cups)
¼ t. salt
1 egg, beaten
1 T. bourbon

When milk gets hot, dissolve butter and sugar in it, and cool. While it cools, dissolve yeast in warm water. Then combine milk mixture, yeast, and eggs. Add raisins. Add this mixture to flour and salt. Let rise until double in size. Loosen from side of bowl, and work into a ball. Make designs on dough, and put on greased pan. Let rise until finger imprint stays on dough. Combine egg and bourbon, and brush on top of dough. Dough is often braided and formed into wreaths. Bake at 350° until top is light brown. Cooking time will vary with size.

Castroville Parisa
Jimmy Burell

1 lb. lean ground beef
½ lb. onions, finely chopped
½ lb. American cheese, finely grated or chopped

lemon juice
salt
pepper

Mix beef, onions (both uncooked), and cheese. Sprinkle small amount of lemon juice over mixture. Taste. Add more if desired. Add salt and pepper to taste. Mix well. Serve on good crisp crackers. Makes 10–12 servings.[11]

followed with café brûlot (coffee with burnt brandy), a drink that gives the host a chance to put on a show.

A French superstition says that a person born on Christmas Day can see spirits. Another says that cattle and horses have the gift of tongues and talk together at Christmastime. But woe to the human who lingers to listen, for he or she will be dead before the year is out!

Traditionally, the holiday season comes to a close for the French with the Feast of the Kings on January 6, Epiphany, which is celebrated with parties and jokes, but not ones as rough as those played by Jean

Chicken and Sausage Gumbo

1 hen, 4–5 lbs.
salt
pepper
onion salt
garlic salt
2 cups shortening

2 cups flour
6 qts. water
2 lbs. smoked sausage
1 bunch green onions, chopped
1 bunch parsley, chopped
2 t. filé

Cut up hen, and season to taste with salt, pepper, onion salt, and garlic salt. Fry in shortening until brown. Remove chicken pieces. Add flour to the same shortening, and stir until dark brown. Add water until roux is dissolved. Bring 6 quarts of water to a strong boil, then drop roux into water gradually. Add hen. Bring to a boil, reduce heat, and cook until hen is tender. Add sausage, and cook 20 minutes. Add green onions and parsley 5 minutes before gumbo is done. Two minutes before gumbo is done, add filé. Serve over rice. Makes 6–8 servings.[12]

Café Brûlot

3 large cups of coffee
1 orange peel
1 lemon peel
6 whole cloves

1 cinnamon stick
8 small sugar lumps
1½ cups brandy

Brew coffee very strong, and keep it very hot. Rinse a brûlot bowl or chafing dish and a silver ladle with boiling water. Cut orange and lemon peels into 1 × ⅛-inch strips. Place peels, cloves, cinnamon, and sugar into bowl, and crush into a somewhat consistent mixture. Mix in brandy. Turn out lights. Ladle out some mixture from bowl, and ignite in the ladle. While blazing, pour back into bowl. Keep ladling mixture in and out of bowl while brandy flames. Add hot coffee, slowly, and continue to ladle mixture until flame dies. Serve in 6 demitasse cups. Take a bow.

Lafitte and his rowdies. Usually there is a cake known as the Cake of the King, which has been baked with a pea and a bean in it. When it is cut, those who receive the pea and the bean get to select the king

and queen of Twelfth Night. From then on, all must obey these mon-
archs who immediately begin to issue ridiculous edicts. In this commemoration, religious feelings and lighthearted gaiety combine, as they
do in all the traditional French *fêtes de Noël*.

X

A Good Witch:

THE ITALIAN HERITAGE

Buon Natale! True to their Catholic heritage, Italians in Texas have always celebrated the Christmas season with a strong religious emphasis, and they continue to resist the secular side of the season. For many Texas Italians the *presepio* (Nativity scene) rather than the Christmas tree represents the spirit of the season.

The first Italian to see Texas may have been Amerigo Vespucci, whose name was given to the New World. There is controversy over whether he actually made the 1497–98 trip that, according to some historians, brought his ships into the Gulf of Mexico. Christopher Columbus, another famous Italian and a contemporary of Vespucci, is honored by the Christopher Columbus Society of San Antonio, which holds monthly spaghetti dinners.

In Texas' fight for independence from Mexico, an Italian, Gen. Vicente Filisola, was second in command to Santa Anna and fought against the Texans. However, another Italian, Prospero Bernardi, helped Texas win independence at San Jacinto.

Beginning in the 1880s, groups of Italians immigrated to the state. They settled in Galveston, Houston, and San Antonio and on farms along the Brazos River. A small group from northern Italy chose to settle in northern Texas near the Red River. Although few in numbers, Texas Italians have made lasting contributions to the arts. Charles A. Siringo wrote *A Texas Cowboy, or Fifteen Years on the Hurricane Deck of a Spanish Pony* (1886) a historically valuable autobiography. In the 1920s Josephine Lucchese became internationally famous as an opera star. And Italian-born sculptor Pompeo Coppini, who came to Texas in 1901, created numerous statues and monuments for his chosen state, including the Littlefield Fountain at the University of Texas and the cenotaph on

Alamo Plaza in San Antonio. In 1889 Adam Janelli, originally from Parma, Italy, brought the Salvation Army to Texas.

Texas Italians, like other immigrants, formed their own organizations and maintained their native traditions to some extent. In some towns they built their own parish churches. The Christmas mass was celebrated with all the pomp and circumstance possible in the raw country.

Saint Francis of Assisi is said to have created the first Nativity scene in Greccio, Italy, in 1223. It was complete with living animals and statues of the Holy Family. The idea quickly caught on, and churches all over Italy began displaying manger scenes. Soon the people adopted the idea and began building *presepios* in their homes as an expression of their joy and reverence at the season of Christ's birth. The custom was brought to Texas where it is still practiced by Italian families.

The scenes may be constructed of marble, wood, cork, plaster, papier-mâché, or other materials and may be rebuilt each year. The purpose of the *presepio* is to reveal the drama of the Nativity. In addition to the Holy Family, the Three Kings, shepherds, angels, flocks of sheep, and cattle are displayed. Local characters can be found in some scenes, wending their way to the sacred grotto, bearing gifts unique to their region.

Christmas Eve is a day of fasting for devout Italians. In the evening a ceremony is held around the *presepio*. Following prayers, the mother places the figure of the bambino, Jesus, in the manger. Traditionally, small Christmas gifts are then distributed from a large crock called the Urn of Fate. Christmas Day is reserved for religious services.

In the tradition brought from Italy to Texas, La Befana comes down the chimney with the more important gifts on Epiphany Eve.[1] The sound of a bell alerts the children that she has paid her annual visit. A pre-Christian sprite, the ancient Roman Befana is sometimes thought of as an aged fairy queen or a good witch. She was incorporated into Christian legends as a stubborn housewife who refused to go with the Magi to seek the Christ Child because she had too much housework to do. When she changed her mind and hurried after the Wise Men, she was unable to find them. Each Epiphany Eve she searches the world for the Holy Infant, stopping to distribute sweets and presents to good Italian children and charcoal or stones to the bad ones. Her name is a corruption of *Epiphania*.

Italian immigrants brought to Texas several lovely carols. "The Carol of the Bagpipers" explains how the brightest star traveled through the sky on the night of Jesus' birth to summon the Wise Men from the Orient to come to the manger. In "Jesus, the New-Born Baby," the infant is crying and Joseph nestles him and sings a soothing refrain, "Loo, loo, my dearest Son."

The words of "From Starry Skies Thou Cometh" lament that the singer cannot supply the infant with physical comforts or gifts:

> . . . appearing in a manger,
> Near frozen from the cold,
> Jesus, dearest little Baby
> How I long to make Thee warm!
> To shelter Thee from harm!
> My heart is filled with pity
> For thy tiny form!
> . . . Jesus, dearest little Baby
> Come in direst poverty,
> Would I had gifts for thee![2]

"Dormi, Dormi, O Bel Bambino" ("Sleep, O Sleep, My Lovely Child") is a traditional Italian lullaby. In the second stanza Mary says:

> O my treasure, do not weep!
> Sweetly sleep, sweetly sleep,
> Close your eyes my Son, my dear one.
> Sweetly sleep, sweetly sleep.
> Close your eyes, my Son, my dear one.[3]

The refrain consists entirely of repetitions of "Fa la la, Fa la."

In 1950, Italian composer Gian Carlo Menotti wrote *Amahl and the Night Visitors,* the first opera commissioned specifically for television. It is the touching story of a lame shepherd boy who gives his crutch to the Magi as a gift for the Christ Child. In addition to being an annual feature on television, the opera is produced in towns and cities all over Texas (and the rest of the nation) by various drama groups, including school children.

A traditional Italian Christmas dinner consists of fish (symbolizing

Christ) and concludes with *panettone,* a sweet breadlike cake filled with fruit and nuts and topped with powdered sugar—a food dating back to the days of the Roman Empire. Pasta in all its delicious varieties frequently appears at festive meals. The Italians also have a way with veal, especially when it is some kind of scaloppine. *Saltimbocca,* literally, jump in the mouth, is well named.[4]

Saltimbocca
(VEAL SCALOPPINE WITH PROSCIUTTO)

8 slices prosciutto or boiled ham	salt
8 veal cutlets, pounded thin	pepper
1 t. sage	3 T. butter

Lay a slice of prosciutto on each cutlet, and sprinkle with sage, salt, and pepper. Do not roll up, but secure meat slices flat with toothpicks inserted at a slant. Sauté meat in butter for 3 minutes on each side. Discard toothpicks. Serve on toast or on a bed of chopped spinach, and garnish with slices of hard-boiled egg, if desired. Serves 4.

Italians are fond of sweets and know how to make delectable desserts. Two holiday favorites are the frothy custard called *zabaglione* and the heavenly concoction known as *tortoni.*

Zabaglione

6 egg yolks	¼ t. cinnamon
⅓ cup sugar	1 cup dry or sweet wine (usually Marsala)

Beat egg yolks, adding sugar gradually, until firm. Add cinnamon and wine slowly, beating well. Set over hot water. Cook and beat until sugar is dissolved and mixture resembles thick custard—about 10 minutes. Serve immediately in sherbet glasses. (To serve cold: beat egg whites separately. When cooked mixture reaches proper consistency, fold in egg whites. Pile in sherbet glasses, and chill.) Serves 6.

Biscuit Tortoni

1 cup heavy cream
¼ cup powdered sugar
1 egg white

½ cup macaroons, crumbled and sieved
1 T. minced cherries
1 T. minced almonds
2 t. sherry

Whip cream. Gradually fold in sugar, stiffly beaten egg white, macaroons, cherries, almonds, and sherry. Pack into individual paper cups. Top with extra macaroon crumbs and colored sugar crystals, if desired. Freeze until firm. Makes 6–8 servings.

A *ceppo* was the early Italian equivalent of the Christmas tree. Somewhat like the German *lichtstock,* it was a cardboard pyramid about three feet high with three or four levels of shelves from bottom to top on which candy, fruit, and small presents were placed.

Asked to decorate a tree for an ethnic display of Christmas trees at the International Holiday Festival held at the Port Arthur Public Library recently, the Italian group displayed a wooden pyramid, festooned with red bows, ropes of beads, and white candles. At the top level on the smallest platform an angel stood guard. Below her a statue of Mary was holding the infant Jesus. On the next level stood figures of the Magi prsenting their gifts to the Christ Child. And at the bottom, on the largest platform, was a complete *presepio* with the star of Bethlehem shining above the manger. Although Italian Texans have incorporated customs from other cultures into their celebrations, it is obvious that they remain mindful of the religious significance of the season.

Festival of the Stars:

THE POLISH HERITAGE

Wesołych Świąt Bozego Narodzenia!

From ancient times, Poles have celebrated Christmas as the Festival of the Stars. When they think of Christmas they think of stars—the star over Bethlehem, "star gifts" brought by the Star Man, star-shaped cookies and tree ornaments, and carolers led by the Star Bearer. Christmas Day itself is known as *Gwiazdka* (little star). And it was under the stars that a group of weary Polish immigrants celebrated their first Christmas midnight mass in Texas in 1854.

After a two-month journey from their homeland of Silesia over rough seas, they had plodded from Galveston to an open knoll fifty-five miles southeast of San Antonio at the confluence of the San Antonio River and Cibolo Creek. There were no houses or buildings of any kind, so the travelers unhitched their carts, laid down their burdens under the trees, and prepared to spend their first night in their new homesite huddled in shallow holes for warmth.

But it was Christmas Eve, *Wigilia* (from Latin *vigilare*, to watch) the most important holiday of the year for Polish people, so at midnight they gathered under the largest oak for the traditional Shepherds' Mass. There in front of a crude altar Father Leopold Moczygemba celebrated the mass and said prayers of thanksgiving for their safe arrival. Then they sang their ancient Christmas carols. They christened their new settlement Panna Maria, the Virgin Mary.

The next year, 1855, the immigrant Poles celebrated Christmas Eve mass in their new church, which was built adjacent to the large oak under which they had held their first celebration. When this church was destroyed by lightning in 1877, it was rebuilt, and in 1937 it was remodeled. For over 135 years this church has been the heart and center of the religious and community life of the Polish pioneers and their descendants who live in the village of Panna Maria.

The Polish settlers who came to Texas to begin their new lives in Panna Maria, Bandera, San Antonio, and other towns throughout the state brought with them colorful and treasured customs, traditions, and beliefs, especially in connection with Christmas. Early in December Polish women begin baking honey spice cakes, *piernik,* since the flavor is enhanced by aging. Formerly the recipes were well-guarded family secrets, which were given to young brides as a part of their dowry. Torun was one of the first cities to add spices to old-time honey cakes, and Torun *piernik* is still famous worldwide. Catherine's order of nuns in Torun attained fame for their honey cakes, which became known as Little Catherines. The cakes can be made in many shapes and forms and traditionally were cooked in hard wood molds. In ancient times *piernik* was believed to have medicinal powers, and sweethearts exchanged the little cakes as tokens of love. Homemakers sprinkled the crumbs of the *piernik* in all the other pans in which Christmas delicacies were baked to bring good luck. Today factories still turn out these tasty little cakes in large quantities. Eventually an inedible form of *piernik* (made into a hard dough without the use of rising compounds) was used to make lasting decorations.

The *piernik* is connected with one of the Polish gift givers, Saint Nicholas or the Frost Man, who visits the homes of good girls and boys in a sneak preview of Christmas on December 6, Saint Nicholas Day. Like many other European people, the Poles have traditionally honored Saint Nicholas, Bishop of Myra in Lycia on the coast of Asia Minor, who is credited with miracles performed both before and after his death. Men posed as Saint Nicholas—they wore long white robes, bishops' miters, and white, flowing beards—and appeared in the cottages of Polish peasants, questioned the children about their behavior, and gave them rewards of heart-shaped *piernik,* holy pictures, and big red apples. The custom continues today.

Centuries before the birth of Jesus, Polish people, along with other Europeans, considered December 24 the last day of the year, and it was an important holiday tied to the solar calendar. Since it was a time to honor Saturn, god of fairness and justice, the celebrations were considered to begin a time of harmony and good will, and that belief carried over into the Christian tradition.

Many Polish superstitions originated in connection with Christmas Eve when it was considered the last day of the year. One of these was the belief that on this day the spirits of the dead visited the homes in which they had lived. It was important to make everything as comfortable as possible for them. Cottages were kept warm, water was provided for washing, and food was set out. Sharp instruments such as needles, knives, and scissors were not brandished in the air or left lying around for fear the wandering spirits might injure themselves. The hope was that, after being made to feel welcome and refreshed, the visiting souls would bless the household.

Another belief was that the last day of the year prophesied everything that would happen in the coming year, so everyone rose early on December 24 to ensure not being lazy during the next year. Hands were washed in a basin of cold water in which a crust of bread and a coin were placed. The crust ensured there would be plenty of bread to sustain life, and the coin ensured that the washer would be strong as metal. Early Texas Poles practiced these beliefs; some present-day Poles can remember going through the rituals with their parents.

When the first star appears in the sky on December 24, the evening rituals of *Wigilia* begin. The father of the house breaks the *oplatek*, a large rectangular wafer, and it is passed along for everyone to break off a piece amid a mutual exchange of good wishes. The *oplatek* symbolizes love, friendship, and forgiveness. Traditionally animals are also given a piece of the *oplatek*. First used in church ceremonies, *oplatki* were sanctioned for lay use during the Middle Ages. The wafers are made of the finest wheat flour and cooked between iron plates similar to waffle irons. Over the years artisans have created beautiful and intricate designs for these irons. Often one side displays a religious scene, such as the stable in Bethlehem, while the other side shows a secular scene, such as a historic Polish building or a Polish farmyard with geese or lambs. Fragile, delicate ornaments are sometimes made from the leftover paper-thin wafers. These may be stars enclosing a tiny cradle with a minute figure of a baby. These lovely decorations are hung by threads from the ceiling or displayed on Christmas trees. *Oplatki* came to be exchanged among the Poles much as Christmas cards are now. Today the wafers are mass-produced in factories as well as being made in homes.

Since the Poles who originally came to Texas were Roman Catholic, Christmas Eve was a fasting day, and no meat was served for the traditional *Wigilia* supper. This custom is still observed, but the meal, nevertheless, is bountiful. It traditionally consists of an uneven number of courses—at least seven, but more often nine or thirteen. Straw is scattered on the table as a reminder of the stable in Bethlehem, and an empty chair is left for the stranger who might appear and be the Christ Child in disguise.

Typically the meal is prepared from foods representing all the sources available to the partakers—crops from the fields, fruit from the orchards, fish from the rivers, and mushrooms from the woods—so the new year will bring a greater harvest of each kind of food. The menu might include fish in horseradish sauce; herring, creamed, cooked in oil, or marinated; beet soup with mushroom-filled dumplings; trout with sauerkraut and mushrooms; dumplings filled with cottage cheese; dried fruit compote; poppyseed rolls; cookies with poppyseeds; honey cake; nut rolls; coffee and tea. Polish dumplings called pierogi are a specialty.[1] This book uses a honey cake recipe from Warsaw.[2]

Elaborate handmade mobiles and chandeliers called spiders preceded the use of Christmas trees in Polish cottages. A Polish custom comparable to the American or English use of mistletoe is the hanging of a *podlaznik*. The tip of a small fir or spruce tree is hung upside down from the ceiling and decorated with apples, nuts, candies, and wafers. *Podlaznik* comes from the term for "sneaking," and it is customary for a young man to try to sneak up behind a girl, catch her under the *podlaznik,* and claim a kiss. On Christmas Day the little tree is lowered and the goodies handed out to the children.

Under German influence, the use of the full-size Christmas tree became popular. The Polish tree was traditionally a stately fir, which was placed in the main room in what was called God's corner, where the favorite holy pictures hung. In Texas the tree was usually a cedar. Handmade decorations are still favored by Poles, especially stars which are made from various materials, such as duck or goose feathers or straw, glued together with clay or candle wax and colored tissue paper.

Since eggs symbolize the miracle of birth, eggshells are also con-

Pierogi

Mrs. James R. Snoga

2 cups flour	2 T. sour cream
½ cup warm milk or water	½ t. salt
1 whole egg plus 1 yolk	1 t. butter, for richer dough

Mix ingredients, and knead into soft pliable dough. Let rest for 10 minutes covered with a warm bowl. Divide dough into halves, and roll thin. Cut circles with large biscuit cutter. Place a small spoonful of filling a little to one side. Moisten edge with water, fold over, and press edges together firmly. Be sure they [the edges] are well sealed. Drop pierogi into salted boiling water. Cook gently for 5 minutes. Lift out carefully with slotted spoon, and serve with melted butter and bread crumbs. Makes 18–20 servings.

FILLINGS

Cheese:

1 cup cottage cheese	3 T. sugar
1 t. melted butter	3 T. currants
1 egg, beaten	1 t. lemon juice

Cream cheese with melted butter. Add other ingredients, and mix well. Fill pierogi.

Sauerkraut and Mushroom:

2 cups sauerkraut	butter
1 small onion, finely chopped	salt
1 cup mushrooms, chopped	pepper

Cook sauerkraut for 10 minutes. Drain, and chop finely. Fry onion and mushrooms in butter. Add kraut, and season with salt and pepper. Fry until flavors are blended. Fill pierogi.

sidered appropriate Christmas decorations. Some of them are intricately adorned with bits of lace, jewelry, and silk threads. A half shell makes a flowerpot for tissue-paper flowers; little pitchers with bases, spouts, and handles of stiff paper and folk-art edging are common. Doves with eggshell bodies symbolize peace, and the eggshell rooster–representing health, fertility, and good luck–is a gay figure on Polish trees with his feet, cockscomb, wings, wattle, eyes, and bright feathered tail all made of stiff paper.

According to an age-old custom, following Christmas Eve supper,

Honey Cake

1 cup sugar	1½ t. cinnamon
3 T. boiling water	1 t. ground cloves
2 T. butter	grated rind of 1 large orange
1 cup honey	4 cups sifted flour
1 cup sour cream	1 t. baking soda
4 large egg yolks	¾ cup seedless raspberry jam
1 t. allspice	1 T. rum

Brown 1 tablespoon sugar in a saucepan. Add water, and stir till dissolved. Add rest of sugar, butter, and honey. Bring to a boil. Remove from heat. Add sour cream, egg yolks, spices, and orange rind. Mix well. Add flour and soda. Beat at medium speed for 5 minutes. Fold into a buttered 9×12-inch pan. Spread evenly. Bake at 350° for about 45 minutes. Let cool. Remove from pan. Cut with a thin, long, sharp knife into two layers. Mix jam with rum, and spread over bottom layer; cover with top layer.

ICING

12 oz. semi-sweet chocolate	½ cup coffee cream
4 T. butter	almonds for decoration

Melt chocolate and butter in cream over low heat. Do not boil. Spread over cake. Decorate with almonds. Refrigerate until set. Cut into long narrow pieces. Keep covered. Cake is better next day.

gifts from the Christmas tree are distributed, and carolers go from house to house singing *koledy,* or carols, some of which can be traced back to medieval times. The religious, serious carols follow a similar pattern: an evangelical revelation followed by a brief exhortation to worship God. A favorite *koledy* is the "Christmas Cradle Hymn." Chopin loved the melody of this beautiful lullaby carol so much that he included it in his *Scherzo in B Minor, Opus 20,* and James Michener refers to it in his book *Poland.* The second stanza says:

Look little wakeful One, Mother is nigh,—
Where stars like silver lamps swing far on high.
　　Dost know, Child, how three kings riding from far,
　　Brought to Thy crib rich gifts, led by Thy star.[3]

Many Polish carols, like English carols, are lighthearted and frivolous. As the Polish carolers went from house to house, children watched eagerly, trying to be the first to spy the star that signified their approach. Attached to long poles, these stars had lighted candles encased in their centers to make the colors of the iridescent paper covering of the star seem to twinkle. Strings, ingeniously attached, could be pulled to make the star twirl rapidly. It was an honor to be chosen as the star carrier to lead the carolers. This old custom is still practiced by some Polish carolers. Since the singers expect to be rewarded with gifts, some of their verses are cajoling:

> May the dear Lord give you
> Success and plenty of health,
> And in the pantry and barn much wealth.
> Dear Lord, give them everywhere
> In the sack, in the field, here, there
> In every corner a tiny tot,
> And near the stove, three more to add to the lot.
> For these good wishes, we would like some cheese,
> Pastry, ham or *kielbasy,* please.
> May the good Lord bless you for it.[4]

The star-led carolers are often accompanied by a comic character called the *turon.* Wearing a heavy wooden mask and dressed in animal skins, he represents a combination of animals, although the name *turon* comes from "tur," a bison, the king of the virgin Polish forests. The *turon* does not speak, but he is full of tricks and practical jokes, and he makes the children squeal with excitement as he dances and crawls on all fours, clapping to keep time to the singing or ringing the small bell around his neck.

The *Pasterka,* or Shepherds' Mass at midnight, is the highlight of *Wigilia.* The services end with the singing of the beloved ancient carols. A young cleric who took part in the midnight mass in 1866 in the old stone church in Panna Maria reported that after the service the people sang carols until they were too hoarse to sing any longer. In many churches the people linger to view the Nativity scenes in the church naves. In Old World cities, especially Krakow and Warsaw, the manger scenes developed into three-tiered elaborate structures that were feats of architecture and which are esteemed as objects of art. But in small churches in Texas the Nativity scenes remained basic, with the kneeling shepherds offering the Christ Child such native gifts as a jar of butter, a piece of cheese, or a lamb. Homes also have manger scenes, often homemade and handed down from generation to generation.

Christmas Day for Polish people has always been a time for the gathering of intimate family groups. Dinner is a feast with meat, usually pork, as its main feature. Polish ham and sausage have become famous and Polish Texans buy them as well as dried Polish mushrooms in city markets.

In contrast to the quiet of the home-centered Polish Christmas Day, the next day—Saint Stephen's Day—is a time for visiting with friends and relatives. The Polish version of an eastern European proverb says, "On the Feast Day of Saint Stephen, there is neither lord nor peasant." This saying refers to the old custom of having the mistress of the house prepare and serve food to the servants, and to the fact that Saint Stephen's was a day to seek new employment, to be hired and to hire. On this day the Poles said: "Everyone is his own master."

New Year's Eve, the feast of Saint Sylvester, is often celebrated with parties in private homes. Like other groups, the Poles have traditionally tried to predict the future as the new year begins. Wax melted and dropped into cold water forms various shapes that are interpreted to predict the person's future. The father blows out a candle and significance is read into the way the smoke goes. If it goes straight up, a prosperous and healthy year is forecast. But smoke going in any other direction bodes ill (which will come from this direction) in the coming year. The Poles practice the same custom as the Czechs on January 6, the Feast of the Three Kings, of using blessed chalk to write the year and the initials of the Three Kings over their doorways as a blessing to their homes.

Since the 1850s Poles have continued to arrive in Texas, individually and in groups. They have spread throughout the state, but there are some areas where they have clustered together and every name is Polish. Such a place is Panna Maria, where the traditions of the homeland are still honored. Here each Christmas Eve the faithful are called to the *Wigilia* mass by the bell brought from a parish church in Silesia. As they file into the old stone church, they pass the ancient oak where

Father Leopold is buried on the spot where he held the first Christmas Eve mass for their ancestors under the stars of the wide Texas sky. Inside the church, as they listen to the same ancient service their ancestors heard and sing the same carols, the Polish Texans remember their heritage.

Cicha nóc - swjata nam nóc!

Rumpliche and Noodles:

THE WENDISH HERITAGE

Wjesoxe Hody! Older Wends in Texas recall the terror and excitement of being visited during Advent by anti–Santa Claus fiends. Rumplich (also known as Knect Ruprecht) was originally a fearsome character whose purpose was literally to scare the devil out of children, whipping those who needed punishment and putting the worst boys in his sack to carry away. Milton Moerby who grew up in the Giddings area remembered:

> When I was a little kid, about this time of year [Advent] there would be a great, loud thumping at the door. It would be Old Man Ruprecht screaming and shouting to be let in. I was scared half to death. But my folks would let him in. Of course it would be a neighbor boy, a young man, dressed up in a Santa Claus suit and wearing an ugly mask, carrying a stick, a whip and a bag. But I thought he was a real monster. Once he tried to put me in his bag. I lost a year's growth, but he couldn't put *me* in that poke![1]

The Rumpliche tradition was carried out in the Giddings-Serbin area until the late 1940s by groups of young men wearing costumes and masks. The usual costume was a white tunic with dark red stripes two or three inches wide, and the masks were black or white cloth with beards made from the long hairs of cows' tails. If a costume was not readily available, however, the young men would put on any kind of tacky dress for their masquerade. Generally eight or ten Rumpliche traveled around together, and another old-timer remembered being "scared out of his wits" when fifteen Rumpliche descended on his house at one time.

Over the years the custom mellowed into a game, reminding everyone of the approach of Christmas, which would bring the adored Christkindchen and blessed Nicholas. Groups of merrymaking Rumpliche went from house to house asking the children if they had been good, spanking their hands if they were mischievous, and sometimes asking them to recite a prayer and then rewarding them with candy, fruit, and nuts. These Rumpliche also sang German Christmas carols and pantomimed to entertain their hosts.

Another cherished tradition among Wends was that the oldest son of the family had the responsibility to gather the barnyard animals and household pets together and repeat to them the story of Christ's birth each Christmas Eve.

Wends are perhaps the least known of all the Texas Pioneers. Ironically, although they fled from their old homeland of Lusatia to escape political and religious oppression by Germans, they have virtually lost their ethnic identity through assimilation with Germanic Texans.[2] Recently, however, the Texas Wendish Heritage Society has made strong efforts to preserve the distinctive Wendish culture. The center for this preservation is in the only Wendish museum in the United States, which was established at Serbin by the society. Nearby is Saint Paul Lutheran Church, the center for community life in the area, as well as a strong reminder of the Wendish pioneers' heroic struggle to survive in their new home.

A few days before Christmas of 1854, the Wendish Moses, Johann Kilian, led his flock of more than five hundred Wends onto Galveston Island. Thankful to leave the "plague ship," on which seventy-three of their number had died from cholera, they saw Galveston as a lovely promised land with blooming oleanders and crape myrtles. But a yellow fever epidemic on the island quickly drove them inland. By oxcart and on foot they trekked to Rabbs Creek, in present-day Lee County, and established the village called Serbin.

The land was stony, and malaria, typhoid, dysentery, and two years of drought hampered their efforts. But they survived, thanks to their close-knit spirit of cooperation and their strong religious faith. Their beloved Lutheran church was the center of their lives. It supplied them with religion, education, entertainment, and a strict moral code. At first, services were held in the two-room log parsonage. But by Christmas of 1859 the hard-working members of the congregation had built themselves a church. On December 25, despite snow and freezing temperatures, the first Wendish church in America was joyfully dedicated at Serbin.

The clear-toned bell that the immigrants had brought with them tolled, and the Reverend Mr. Kilian led the Wendish church members and their friends from the parsonage into the new church building. He preached three sermons: one in Wendish, one in German for the German visitors, and one in English for the Americans who attended the service. This service was a memorable event in the history of the Wendish pioneers, and appropriately it included the singing of many old carols in the Wendish tongue.

Easter and Christmas are the two great holidays for the Wends, and each calls for three days of festivities. In earlier days, preparation for Christmas began soon after Thanksgiving, but not by shopping for gifts. It was time to decide which hogs were to be fattened so they could be butchered to make lard for baking and smoked ham and sausage. The Christmas goose was literally stuffed with cornmeal balls made with rich milk until it could hardly waddle. The Wends washed the walls and even the ceilings of their houses in preparation for celebrating the Lord's birthday. If the weather permitted, they also washed windows, curtains, and quilts. During the second week in December the baking started. Fruitcakes, *stritzel* (Christmas bread), and *pfeffernause* cookies all needed aging.

The first week in December the children began practicing for the Christmas Eve program. Religious pageants and recitations by the schoolchildren were featured in special church services that often lasted two or three hours. A tall cedar decorated with different colored beeswax candles and other handmade ornaments stood in front of the church. As German and English replaced Wendish, the children sang "Der Christbaum ist der Schoenste Baum," "Gott ist die Liebe," and "O Come All Ye Faithful," among other Christmas songs. Older children recited Old Testament passages concerning the coming of the Savior, and the younger children recited short poems about Jesus' birthday. Each child received a brown paper sack filled with fruit, nuts, candy, and a religious story book.

Christmas trees in homes were decorated by the older members of the family behind locked doors, and the younger children believed that

Rumplich did the decorating. The trimmings were mainly apples and oranges, decorated cookies, candy in shiny white paper wrappers with fine colored fringe, and religious pictures with Bible verses on them. The children did not receive or expect elaborate gifts. Dolls or new clothes for old dolls pleased the girls, and the boys were satisfied with new shirts or caps and sometimes a simple toy. The emphasis of the season was on religious services, fellowship, games, singing, and feasting.

New Year's, too, was a time for religious observance and for feasting. Some Wendish families today follow the tradition of welcoming in the New Year by eating herring for health, black-eyed peas for wealth, and mashed potatoes for happiness. Others enjoy baked ham, smoked sausage, and homemade sauerkraut. Wine made from wild grapes and eggnog with a little whiskey provides the means for making toasts to the New Year after the family returns from church services on December 31.

During the holiday season the famous Wendish noodles are consumed in great quantities. The Wendish Heritage Society provided the recipe given in this chapter.

Coffee cake is a favorite holiday food of many Wendish Texans, and many of them have treasured family recipes, such as the one below. Often the coffee cake is topped with cottage cheese or with a streusel topping, and for the holidays it may have both.[3]

Wendish Noodles

3 eggs	¼ t. salt
2 T. water	2½ cups flour

Beat eggs, add water, salt, and about 2¼ cups flour to make stiff dough. Let stand 10–20 minutes. Make 5 balls of dough, and use rest of flour to roll dough very thin. Let dry on table until they will not stick together when stacked. Cut into 2-inch strips, stack, and cut in desired width with a very sharp knife. Cook 3 cups of the above noodles in 4 cups of boiling stock (either chicken or beef bouillon cubes may be used). Boil noodles for 10 minutes or longer, but do not overboil. Add 1 tablespoon of butter or margarine, after draining noodles. Chopped parsley, chopped green onion tops, and a dash of nutmeg may be added for flavor.

Wendish Coffee Cake

1 package dry yeast	4 T. melted butter
2½ cups warm water	1 cup sugar
1 T. sugar	1 egg
flour (about 2 cups)	½ t. salt
1 cup warm milk	flour (about 4 cups)

Mix yeast, water, and 1 tablespoon sugar, and let rise 10 minutes. Add enough flour (about 2 cups) to make a soft dough. Let rise 30 minutes. Add warm milk, butter, 1 cup sugar, egg, salt, and about 4 cups flour. Work to a medium stiff dough, and let rise in a warm draft-free place until double in size. Flatten on cookie sheet; let rise again to double. Put toppings on, and bake at 350° for 15 minutes.

COTTAGE CHEESE TOPPING

1 pt. cottage cheese	1 or 2 eggs, well-beaten
2 T. cream	1 t. vanilla or ½ t. lemon extract
a little salt	pinch or two of nutmeg
¼ cup sugar	

Press cottage cheese dry in a cheesecloth bag, and crumble it thoroughly. Combine all ingredients. Mixture should not be runny, but should be soft enough to spread on dough.

STREUSEL TOPPING

½ cup butter	pinch of salt
½ cup sugar	a little nutmeg
1 cup flour	

Beat butter and sugar until foamy. Add flour, salt, and nutmeg, and mix with fork until crumbly. Spread on dough.

For the Texas Wends, Santa Claus has replaced *Rumplich,* and the children expect and receive more gifts. But the celebration of the Christmas season is still centered around the good life associated with home and church.

A Harmonious Diversity:

THE ORTHODOX HERITAGE

Sretan Božič! The Orthodox Church has deep and lasting roots in Christian antiquity and a rich heritage of biblical tradition. In 1054 when the great split between Rome and Constantinople occurred, the Western Slavs became Roman Catholic and the Eastern group remained in the Orthodox Church. Today there are some 225 million Orthodox Christians worldwide and over six million in the United States. The federation of Orthodox churches (which are independent in operation but united by common beliefs and traditions) is sometimes called the Greek Church. There are fifteen Orthodox parishes in Texas today.

Advent in the Orthodox Church is a time of fasting—to cleanse the body in preparation for celebrating Christ's birth. Christmas services are held at midnight on Christmas Eve or on Christmas morning, depending on the wishes of the congregation and the pastor. Children's pageants, relating the Nativity story or other Christmas themes, are accompanied by Christmas hymns and carols. These are usually sung in English, but there may be one Greek or Lebanese song. Favorites are "The Lord Has Sent Redemption," "Hymn of St. Nicholas," and "Your Birth O Christ," which begins "Your birth O Christ did shine upon the world and through the light of wisdom illumined the universe."

Long before Greeks begans immigrating to Texas in the late nineteenth and early twentieth centuries, Greek Revival architecture had reached the state. By the mid-nineteenth century, a number of stately antebellum homes, including the Governor's Mansion in Austin, had been built in the Greek Revival style. Some of these mansions in Houston, Jefferson, San Augustine, and other cities are beautifully decorated in Victorian Christmas style and open to the public for tours during the holidays each year.

The earliest Greek pioneers to venture to Texas were sailors and fishermen who brought along their colorful folklore about Greek Christmas ghosts. These ghosts (*kallikantzaree*) spend most of the year underground, hacking away with axes, trying to cut down the tree of life. Just as it is about to fall, Christ is born, and the tree regains its strength. This makes the Greek ghosts furious, and they leap up on earth to become pests.

Professor Helen Cominos, who teaches modern Greek, has described their antics:

> Greek Christmas ghosts slip into houses through the chimney. They are very noisy, dancing, jumping, hopping and wandering about everywhere. Some try to put out the fire in the fireplace, others force people to dance against their will. Some sit on people's shoulders or ride horseback-like on them. They pollute the food. They purloin delicious Christmas sweets and pastries. . . . Greek Christmas ghosts are terrible pests, a pain in the neck. But they never hurt anyone. And since their eyesight is so bad and so stupid are they, real people can easily get the better of them.[1]

Greek families take different measures to protect themselves from these ornery creatures. Some try to coax the ghosts with sweets and honey cakes. Others throw salt and old shoes into the fireplace on Christmas Eve, hoping the crackling of the salt and the odor of burning leather will cause the ghosts to take flight.

There is no consensus about what the ghosts look like, but they are said to be extremely ugly, hairy, dark, skinny or squatty, with red eyes and cleft hooves. Most stories say they have poor eyesight and are stupid. In addition to sweets, their favorite foods are worms, frogs, and snakes. All legends agree that on January 6, Epiphany, when holy water is sprinkled in their direction, they run off screaming to their underground hideouts to begin chopping away at the tree of life again.

New Year's Day, Saint Basil's Day, is the traditional gift-giving time for Greeks, and it is still observed by some Texans, especially those who have recently come from Greece.[2] The majority of Greek Texans, however, have adopted the American Santa who delivers gifts on Christmas Eve. A still popular Greek New Year's tradition is to bake a coin (originally a gold piece, but today usually a shiny dime) in a rich bread called New Year's bread. The first piece of bread is for God, the second is for the church, and the third is for the family. The next piece is given to the oldest member of the family, the next to the second oldest, and so on down to the youngest. The receiver of the coin is considered to be lucky.

Olive oil and spices are used generously in Greek cooking. *Dolmathes,* grape leaves stuffed with well-seasoned ground beef and rice, are popular during the holidays. Lemons grow large and juicy in Greece, and honey is a favorite sweetening. Greek Texans, who have brought along their treasured recipes, might begin the Christmas Eve meal with Greek lemon soup and end it with the melting sweetness of baklava.

Avgolemono (Lemon Soup)
Susan Pepps

2 lbs. chicken parts	3 qts. water
1 onion	½ cup rice
1 stalk celery	2 eggs, separated
1 carrot	2 T. lemon juice
	2 t. salt

Boil chicken with onion, celery, and carrot in water until tender. Remove chicken. Strain broth, and return to pan. Add rice, and simmer about 15 minutes or until tender. Beat egg whites until stiff. Add yolks, and beat well. Adding lemon juice and salt slowly, continue beating mixture. Gradually add to broth, beating constantly to prevent curdling. Return to heat, but do not allow to boil. Pieces of chicken may be added to soup, or it may be roasted and served separately. Serve soup with a slice of lemon. Makes 10–12 servings.

In the 1880s immigrants began coming to Texas from the small republics that became Yugoslavia. In 1901 a Yugoslav Texan, Anthony Francis Lucas, gave his adopted state a spectacular New Year's present. The fabulous Lucas Gusher blew in at Spindletop near Beaumont on January 10, 1901. This marked the beginning of Texas' importance as an oil-producing state and marked the formation of the Texas Company, the Gulf Oil Corporation, and hundreds of other oil companies. It was the

Baklava

2 lbs. chopped walnuts
1 t. cinnamon
½ t. ground cloves

¾ lb. butter, melted
1 lb. phyllo (filo) pastry sheets

SYRUP

½ pt. honey
¼ t. lemon extract

1 lb. sugar
juice of half a lemon

Combine walnuts and spices. Brush bottom of 10×14-inch baking dish with melted butter. Place 1 pastry sheet in dish. Brush with melted butter. Repeat process with 3 more pastry sheets. Sprinkle with nut mixture. Add four more layers of pastry, brushing each with butter. Again sprinkle with nut mixture. Repeat process until all of nut and spice mixture is used. End with 4 layers of phyllo pastry brushed with butter. Cut into diamond shapes. Bake at 300° until golden brown, about 20 minutes. While pastry is baking, boil syrup ingredients together. Cool. Using a spoon, pour very slowly over warm baked baklava.

start of the modern petroleum industry. Today Lucas's contributions to Texas continue through the Anthony Francis Lucas Foundation, a charitable fund to care for children and to advance scholarship.

Many of the Yugoslav immigrants settled in Galveston, where they founded Saints Constantine and Helen Serbian Orthodox Church. This church has carefully preserved the traditional rituals and festivities of the Yugoslav Christmas celebration. The observances fall on January 6 and 7, in accordance with the Julian Calendar. On Christmas Eve, the Day of the Oak (*Badnji Dan*), a special oak (the *badnjak*) is felled. The man who cuts the tree fells it to the east and recites ritual lines to show respect for it. The tree is not touched by bare hands, but is handled reverently by men wearing gloves. The tree is cut into three pieces. The lowest section is the Yule log, which is burned behind the church in remembrance of the fires built by the shepherds in the hills overlooking Bethlehem. The middle section (the *badnjacica*) is called the female Yule log, and after it is decorated, it is placed in the fellowship hall. The top branches and twigs (the *badnjzcici*) are called the children of the Yule log. These are carried home to be placed on the image of each family's patron saint. A small tree, decorated with cookies, nuts, apples, and red, white, and blue streamers is placed in the sanctuary.

After Christmas Eve vespers service in the sanctuary, the congregation gathers in the fellowship hall for light refreshments to break their fast. No meat or dairy products are served, but hot plum brandy and a special bread, dried fruits, and cooked vegetables are offered. Then the female log from the fellowship hall and the small decorated tree from the sanctuary are thrown on the Yule fire behind the church. The children are allowed to snatch the edible goodies from the trees before the fire devours them.

On Christmas Day there is a church service, and then the family goes home to share a special cake (the *cesnica*), which has a silver coin baked in it. The coin represents good luck for the person who finds it.

During the Christmas observance the floors of the church are strewn with straw as a reminder of Jesus' birth in a stable. A story dating back to early Slavic days tells of the spiritual significance of straw. To allow them to take part in the grace of Jesus' humble birth, small children did not sleep in their own beds on Christmas Eve. Instead they were put on a bed of straw. As a further reminder that all the joys of this holiday originated from the birth of Jesus, straw is spread around the Christmas trees in the homes and on the floors of the houses. Straw decorations have long been favorites with Slavic people. In the Middle Ages most were designed with religious symbolism and some still are, but straw is also used for wreaths, centerpieces, and small decorative figures. A special Yugoslavian holiday treat is a multilayered coffee bread with a walnut filling.

Syrian and Lebanese Orthodox Christians have immigrated to Texas since the late nineteenth century.[3] Today Syrian and Lebanese Texans are dispersed throughout the state from El Paso to Beaumont. In these cities and in others such as Waco, Houston, San Antonio, and Austin, they hold festive get-togethers called *sahrias* with music of lutes, hand drums, and tambourines. To the wailing, haunting half tones of the Arabic music, they dance the *dabke,* the traditional circle dance.

Kibbee, a dish made of ground lamb or beef mixed with spices, is sure to star at their holiday meals. It is popular served either raw or baked. Another favorite is cabbage rolls stuffed with ground beef and spices. Yogurt, too, appears in many variations. Long before yogurt

Potica (Christmas Bread)

3½ cups all-purpose flour	2 T. butter
1 package dry yeast	1 t. salt
1 cup milk	1 egg
2 T. sugar	

WALNUT FILLING

2 cups walnuts, ground	2 T. milk
1 egg, beaten	1 T. butter, melted
¼ cup brown sugar, packed	1 t. cinnamon
2 T. honey	½ t. almond extract

Place 1½ cups flour and yeast in large mixer bowl, and stir. Heat milk, sugar, butter, and salt until warm (115°–120°), stirring constantly until butter melts. Add to dry mixture; add egg. Beat at low speed for 30 seconds, scraping bowl. Beat 3 minutes at high speed. Stir in enough of the remaining flour to make a moderately stiff dough. Turn out onto large floured cloth. Knead 6–8 minutes. Place in greased bowl, and turn over. Let rise until double, about 1 hour. Mix together walnut filling ingredients. Set aside. Punch dough down. Cover and let rest 10 minutes. On floured cloth, roll dough to ¼-inch thickness, about 25×10 inches. Stretch gently, working from center to edges, pulling very thin, to about 30×20 inches. Spread with walnut filling. Starting at long side, use cloth as guide to roll up, jelly-roll fashion. Pinch edge to seal. Place one end of roll in center of large greased baking sheet. Coil dough to make snail-shaped spiral; seal end. Cover; let rise in warm place until nearly double, 30–45 minutes. Bake at 350° for 30–35 minutes, until golden brown.

became a popular American food, it was served morning, noon, and night in Syria and Lebanon.

Saint Nicholas Orthodox Church in Waco is a small red brick building surmounted by a Greek cross. Inside it provides a feast for the senses. An icon of St. Nicholas in the vestibule is surrounded by flowers and honored by the worshippers as they enter the church. Inside the nave are more gilt icons of the Virgin Mary with her Child, of Christ, of the Apostles, and of other holy and heroic Christians of the past. These icons are visual aids in worship and dramatic reminders that there is more to reality than what can be seen on earth; they are "windows to heaven."

Incense is used in Orthodox worship to honor the presence of the

Divine. The altar is censed because it represents the throne of God. The icons are censed because they depict God's Son and His saints. The people are censed because each of them is made in the image of God. Through the use of incense, the people are called to worship.

On Christmas, ministers in rich, gold brocade robes conduct the Divine Liturgy in the glow of flickering candles in red holders. The small, well-trained choir sings the litanies and hymns in perfect harmony, and the congregation joins in. Incense fills the air and decorations of greenery and flowers add to the beauty of the service.

Saint Nicholas Church extends a warm welcome to people of all faiths. Although regular members number fewer than a hundred, the church is filled to overflowing on most Sundays and especially during the Christmas season. In addition to Texas Greeks, Texans of Ukrainian, Yugoslavian, Armenian, Russian, and other descents fill the pews.

Just before the main part of the Liturgy, the eucharistic offering, the people embrace and exchange kisses in accordance with Saint Paul's counsel to "greet each other with a holy kiss." This gesture affirms that they are at peace with God and at peace with each other.

By its name, Saint Nicholas Church reminds us of the saint from whom Santa Claus and the secular side of Christmas evolved. And through its spirit of love and brotherhood, it is a reminder of the spiritual significance of the season and of the rich diversity of cultures that are mingled in Texas' celebration of Christmas.

Notes

CHAPTER I, *Texas Celebrates*

1. Henri Joutel, *Joutel's Journal of La Salle's Last Voyage,* p. 77.

2. A group of about thirty Texans planned to divide Texas between a republic called Fredonia and the Indians, in return for Indian help in their rebellion against Mexico and local authorities.

3. D. W. C. Baker, comp., *A Texas Scrap Book,* p. 72.

4. Robert Hancock Hunter, *Narrative of Robert Hancock Hunter, 1813–1902,* ed. B. G. Green, pp. 11–12.

5. Mary Austin Holley to Mrs. William M. Brand, Dec. 20, 1837, Holley Papers, Barker Texas History Center, University of Texas, Austin.

6. Mary Austin Holley to Mrs. William M. Brand, Jan. 1, 1938. Holley Papers.

7. Austin *Daily Bulletin,* quoted in Walter Prescott Webb, "Christmas and New Year in Texas," *Southwestern Historical Quarterly* 44 (Jan., 1941): 366–67.

8. Frederick L. Olmsted, "Scraps of Newspaper," in *A Journey through Texas: Saddle-Trip on the Southwestern Frontier,* p. 497.

9. Ferdinand Roemer, *Texas: With Particular Reference to German Immigration* trans. Oswald Mueller, p. 48.

10. *The Age,* Wallisville, Tex. (Dec., 1986).

11. Ella K. Stumpf, "Christmas in Old San Antonio," San Antonio *Express-News,* Dec. 23, 1983.

12. Katherine Hart, "Julia Pease's Christmastime Included Love and Patience," *Austin American-Statesman,* Dec. 18, 1971.

13. Elizabeth B. Custer, *Tenting on the Plains; or, General Custer in Kansas and Texas* pp. 245–47.

14. Henderson Shuffler, "'Dixie' Becomes a Yule Song," *Houston Chronicle,* Dec. 24, 1973.

15. Audrey Bateman, "Newspapers of a Century Past Reflect Holiday Spirit," *Austin American-Statesman,* Dec. 16, 1988.

16. Mary D. Farrell and Elizabeth Silverthorne, *First Ladies of Texas* (Belton: Stillhouse Publishers Inc., 1978), p. 93.

17. Kenneth Foree, "When a New Year Meant Champagne," *Dallas Morning News,* Jan. 1, 1952.

18. S. Omar Barker, "Oldtime Christmas Gallyhoot," *Cattleman,* Dec., 1953, p. 32.

19. Henderson Shuffler, "Pioneer Celebrations–Rambunctious–But Human," Goliad Texas *Express,* Dec. 22, 1963.

CHAPTER II, *Posadas, Pastores, and Piñatas*

1. Ella K. Daggett Stumpf, "Christmas in Old San Antonio," *Magazine of San Antonio,* Dec., 1977, p. 63.

2. The *posadas* ceremony with its accompanying songs was also introduced into Texas by a group of Canary Islanders who arrived in 1731. Thus Christmas carols were brought into Texas in Spanish long before they were introduced in English by Anglo-American immigrants.

3. Walter Ehret and George K. Evans, comps., *The International Book of Christmas Carols,* p. 307.

4. Ibid., pp. 256–57.

5. In New Mexico a distinction is made between small piñon bonfires, called *luminarias,* and candles in paper bags, called *farolitos.*

6. Ann Maria Watson, "Tales of Christmas Past," *Magazine of San Antonio,* Dec., 1978, p. 58.

7. Ibid.

CHAPTER III, *Hardscrabble Christmas*

1. Florence Fenley, *Oldtimers of Southwest Texas,* p. 16.

2. Charles F. Taylor to James H. Starr, Dec. 24, 1839, Starr Papers, Barker Texas History Center, University of Texas.

3. Frederick Law Olmsted, *A Journey through Texas: A Saddle-Trip on the Southwestern Frontier,* pp. 68–69.

4. Jack Elgin, "Christmas Dinner on the Upper Brazos in 1872," *West Texas Historical Association Year Book* 14 (Oct., 1938): 89–90.

5. James B. Gillett, *Six Years with the Texas Rangers: 1875–1881,* ed. Milo Milton Quaife, p. 57.

6. The german was an intricate French dance performed in a circle. After it was replaced in popularity by newer dances, it continued to be a term used for dance parties.

7. Lee Simmons, "Observations on Horses across Seventy-Five Years," *Southwestern Historical Quarterly* 58 (Oct., 1954): 212–13.

8. Adolphus Sterne, *Hurrah for Texas! The Diary of Adolphus Sterne 1838–1851,* ed. Archie P. McDonald, pp. 20–22.

9. William Bollaert, *William Bollaert's Texas,* ed. W. Eugene Hollon and Ruth Lapham Butler, p. 295.

10. J. B. Polley, "Historical Reminiscences," n.d. DRT Library, Alamo, San Antonio, Texas.

11. Larry Chittenden, "The Cowboys' Christmas Ball," *Austin American-Statesman* Dec. 5, 1956.

12. William A. Owens, *Tell Me a Story, Sing Me a Song:* A Texas Chronicle pp. 111–12.

13. Willam Bollaert, *William Bollaert's Texas,* p. 295.

14. Fenley, *Oldtimers,* pp. 47–48.

15. Ralph Semmes Jackson, *Home on the Double Bayou: Memories of an East Texas Ranch,* p. 57.

16. Ibid., p. 60.

17. Harry H. Campbell, *The Early History of Motley County,* pp. 60–61.

18. Wayne Gard, "Simple Christmas Enlivened Frontier," *Dallas Morning News* Dec. 25, 1952.

19. Chaplains' Reports, Dec. 25, 1884. Typescript of MF-13, Roll #94. Fort Concho Library, San Angelo.

20. There is a question as to whether Moore was the author of the original poem. Some scholars think the poem was written by Henry Livingston, Jr.

21. *Excelsior House Cookbook,* comp. Jessie Allen Wise Garden Club, Jefferson, Texas (Marshall, Tex.: Demmer Co.), 1972, p. 74.

CHAPTER IV, *Keeping the Faith*

1. George P. Rawick: ed., *The American Slave: A Composite Autobiography,* series 2, Texas Narratives: Andrew Moody, p. 1116.

2. Ibid., John Price, p. 2131.

3. Katherine Hart, "Holiday Happenings in Early Day Texas," *Texas Star* (Nov. 12, 1972), p. 2.

4. William Bollaert, *William Bollaert's Texas,* ed. W. Eugene Hollon and Ruth Lapham Butler, pp. 293, 299–300.

5. Adapted from Walter Ehret and George K. Evans, comps., *The International Book of Christmas Carols,* p. 86.

6. Ibid., p. 84–85.

7. Ibid., p. 83.

8. Ibid., p. 82.

9. *The Melting Pot: Ethnic Cuisine in Texas,* p. 10.

10. *All about Kwanza: an African Celebration,* pamphlet.

CHAPTER V, *O Tannenbaum*

1. Gustav Dresel, *Gustav Dresel's Houston Journal,* pp. 90–92.

2. Ferdinand Roemer, *Texas,* p. 51.

3. The hand-carved figures of the Ervendbergs, their children, and the orphans have an interesting history. Many of them were made in East Germany

by a family the Timmermanns had heard about through mutual friends. They were fashioned after the descriptions in a copy of Hermann Seele's diary, which was smuggled into Soviet-occupied East Germany, soon after World War II. It was a tricky business getting the figures back to Texas. In payment the artists asked only for tobacco, sugar, and stockings–more valuable than American cash would have been at that time.

4. Samuel Wood Geiser, *Naturalists of the Frontier,* pp. 141–43.

5. Danette Knopp, "Frohe Weinachten!" *Texas Hill Country View* (Jan., 1989). The Advent calendar was also popular with German families, perhaps because it kept children patient as they opened a different window each day before Christmas.

6. Julia Estill, "Customs among the German Descendants of Gillespie County," *Coffee in the Gourd,* ed. J. Frank Dobie, p. 71.

7. Gilbert J. Jordan, *Yesterday in the Texas Hill Country,* p. 120.

8. Walter Ehret and George K. Evans, comps., *International Book of Christmas Carols,* pp. 138–39.

9. Prang also added color to American lives in other ways. Many Texas children have grown up carrying flat boxes of Prang water colors and fat Prang crayons in their school bags.

10. Leslie Daiken, *Children's Toys throughout the Ages* p. 131.

11. Jordan, *Yesterday,* p. 120.

12. Hermann Seele, *The Cypress and Other Writings of a German Pioneer in Texas,* trans. Edward C. Breitenkamp, pp. 47–48.

CHAPTER VI, *Dickens of a Christmas*

1. R. H. Williams, *With the Border Ruffians; Memories of the Far West, 1852–1868,* ed. E. W. Williams, p. 206.

2. Charles Dickens, *The Pickwick Papers,* pp. 350–51.

3. John E. Baur, *Christmas on the American Frontier, 1800–1900,* 250–51.

4. Mary J. Jaques, *Texan Ranch Life,* pp. 229–30.

5. William Bollaert, *William Bollaert's Texas,* ed. W. Eugene Hollon and Ruth Lapham Butler, p. 293.

CHAPTER VII, *Kolaches, Polkas, and Blessed Chalk*

1. *Vánočni noc,* typescript. SPJST Museum, Temple, Texas.

2. The nation of Czechoslovakia was not created until 1918.

3. Walter Ehret and George K. Evans, comps., *The International Book of Christmas Carols,* p. 226.

4. Recipe for kolaches from *The Melting Pot: Ethnic Cuisine in Texas,* pp. 41–42.

5. Marie Rosický, *Bohemian American Cookbook* (Privately printed, 1906).

6. The European carp differs from the American carp. It may grow to thirty pounds or more and is highly esteemed.

7. *Melting Pot,* pp. 43–44.

8. In West, "a son whose candle sputtered out was drowned shortly afterward." Olga Pazdral, "Czech Folklore in Texas," Master's thesis, University of Texas, 1942, p. 175.

9. Olga Pozdral, "Some Czech Christmas Traditions and Superstitions," *Naše Dějiny* (Hallettsville, Tex.), Nov.–Dec., 1983, p. 5.

CHAPTER VIII, *Barnfests and Lutefisk*

1. Walter Ehret and George K. Evans, comps., *The International Book of Christmas Carols,* p. 193.

2. In 1963 it cost ninety cents a pound; today it is thirteen dollars a pound.

3. George Carmack, "Norwegian Christmas Dinner Is Not the Usual, but Lutefisk," San Antonio *Express-News,* Dec. 14, 1974.

CHAPTER IX, *Père Noël*

1. Lafitte's father was French; his mother Spanish. He was born in Bayonne, France.

3. Dr. J. O. Dyer, "Holiday Season in Early Texas," *Galveston Daily News* (Dec. 26, 1920).

3. Ibid.

4. Kenneth Hafertepe, *A History of the French Legation in Texas,* Isaac Van Zandt to Mrs. Isaac Vandt, Dec. 6, 1840, p. 7.

5. Bengal fire or light is a kind of colored fire used in theaters and in signaling. It is composed of potassium, nitrate, sulphur, and antimony.

6. Emmanuel Henri Domenech, *Missionary Adventures in Texas and Mexico: A Personal Narrative of Six Years' Sojourn in Those Regions,* pp. 185–87.

7. Ibid., pp. 350–51.

8. Walter Ehret and George K. Evans, comps., *The International Book of Christmas Carols,* p. 327.

9. Ibid., pp. 112–13.

10. Castro Colonies Heritage Association, *Old Favorite Receipts,* unpaginated.

11. Ibid.

12. *The Melting Pot: Ethnic Cuisine in Texas,* p. 88.

CHAPTER X, *Good Witch*

1. Epiphany originally celebrated both the birth and baptism of Jesus, but since the fourth century, it has marked especially the arrival of the Three Wise Men, or Magi, at the stable in Bethlehem.

2. Walter Ehret and George K. Evans, comps., *The International Book of Christmas Carols,* pp. 244–45.

3. Ibid., pp. 248–49.

4. Lone Star Gas Co., Home Economics Dept., *Festival of Gas World Cookbook,* pamphlet, p. 3.

CHAPTER XI, *Festival of the Stars*

1. *The Melting Pot: Ethnic Cuisine in Texas,* pp. 174–75.

2. Alina Zeranska, "Traditional Polish Christmas Eve Supper," *Naród Polski* (Dec. 8, 1983), p. 8.

3. Saint Mary's Church, *Christmas Carols and Polish Koledy,* booklet.

4. *The Treasured Polish Christmas Customs and Traditions,* (New York: Kosciusko Foundation, 1971), p. 27.

CHAPTER XII, *Rumpliche and Noodles*

1. Victor Vogel, "Wendish Christmas," *Free and Easy* (Clipping file, Texas Wendish Heritage Museum, n.d.), p. 5.

2. The Wends actually are Slavs; their language resembles Czech and Polish more than it does German.

3. Dora Weiser Fischer, *As I Remember,* pp. 159–60.

CHAPTER XIII, *Harmonious Diversity*

1. Helen Cominos, "Greek Christmas Ghosts Scream the Loudest," *Orthodox Observer* (December, 1980), pp. 6–7.

2. Saint Basil was a bishop in the fourth century who educated himself by traveling about the monasteries of Egypt, Palestine, and Syria. He established hospitals and cared for the poor and homeless. His writings were vast.

3. They were called Syrians until the Ottoman Empire was broken up in 1919, and Lebanon emerged as a separate nation.

Bibliography

Unpublished Material

Castroville Public Oral History Project. Alsatian Customs and Traditions. Interviews with Molly Hans Schott, Florence Lamon Tschirhart, and Ralph L. Tschirhart.

Clarke, Laura. Papers. Barker Texas History Center, University of Texas, Austin.

Crimmins, Col. M. L. Papers. Eberstadt Collection, Barker Texas History Center, University of Texas, Austin.

Fort Clark Records. Barker Texas History Center, University of Texas, Austin.

Fort Duncan Records. Barker Texas History Center, University of Texas, Austin.

Fort Elliott Records. Barker Texas History Center, University of Texas, Austin.

Grierson Family Papers. Tom Green County Historical Society. Duplicate copies in Research Library and Archives, Fort Concho National Historic Landmark, San Angelo.

Holley, Mary Austin. Papers. Barker Texas History Center, University of Texas, Austin.

Maxey, Rella. Diary, 1858–1860. Star of the Republic Museum, Washington, Texas.

Newcomb, S. E., and S. P. Newcomb. Papers. Barker Texas History Center, University of Texas, Austin.

Pazdral, Olga. "Czech Folklore in Texas." Master's thesis, University of Texas, 1942.

"A Report on The Hygiene of the United States Army, with Descriptions of Military Posts," Circular No. 8, May 1, 1875, Fort McKavett Library.

Starr, James H. Papers. Barker Texas History Center, University of Texas, Austin.

"Vánočni noc." Typescript. SPJST Museum, Temple, Texas.

Warner, Lucy Rawlings. "Fort Concho, Texas–1867 to 1889." Master's thesis, University of Arizona, 1939.

Williams, Mary. "Christmas at Fort Davis." Typescript. Archives, Fort Davis National Historic Site.

United States. *A NJ and Gazette of the Regular Army Forces,* 1884–85. Bound vols. 22 and 23 of *United States Army Navy Journal.* Archives, Fort Davis, Texas.

Books and Articles

Abernethy, Francis Edward, ed. *The Folklore of Texan Cultures.* Austin: Encino Press, 1974.

All about Kwanza: an African Celebration. Brooklyn: The East, n.d. Pamphlet.

Alter, Judy, and Joyce Gibson Roach. *Texas and Christmas: A Collection of Traditions, Memories and Folklore.* Fort Worth: Texas Christian University Press, 1983.

Andrews, Brad, "A Dickens of a Christmas." *Southwest Airlines Magazine,* December 1979, pp. 46–51.

Aniol, Claude B. "Stories Recalled of Christmas Past in Old San Antonio." *North San Antonio Times,* December 23, 1971.

———. "Texas' First Christmas Tree." *North San Antonio Times,* December 25, 1978.

"At Number of Churches Christmas is Observed." *Austin American-Statesman,* December 28, 1904.

"Auld Lang Syne as She Is Sung." Edinburgh *Scotsman,* December 31, 1979.

Baca, Marie. *Memorial Book and Recipes.* Privately printed, 1957.

Baker, D. W. C., comp. *A Texas Scrap Book Made Up of the History, Biography and Miscellany of Texas and Its People.* Austin: Steck Co., 1935.

Baker, T. Lindsay. *The First Polish Americans: Silesian Settlements in Texas.* College Station: Texas A&M University Press, 1979.

Barker, S. Omar. "Oldtime Christmas Gallyhoot." *Cattleman,* December, 1953, p. 32.

Bateman, Audrey. "Newspapers of a Century Past Reflect Holiday Spirit." *Austin American-Statesman,* December 16, 1988.

———. "A Nostalgic Glimpse of Holidays Gone By." *Austin American-Statesman,* December 25, 1985.

Baur, John E. *Christmas on the American Frontier, 1800–1900.* Caldwell, Idaho: Caxton Printers, 1961.

Beverly, Bob. "Christmas at Midland, Texas, in the Early 1890's." *Cattleman,* January, 1951, p. 28.

Biesele, R. L. "Prince Solm's Trip to Texas, 1844–1845." *Southwestern Historical Quarterly* 40 (July, 1936): 20.

Bishop, Curtis. "Christmas at Perote." *Texas Parade,* December, 1954, p. 17.

———. "The Christmas Tree Comes to Texas." *Texas Parade,* December, 1952, pp. 24–25.

———. "Merry Christmas." *Texas Co-op Power,* December, 1954.

———. "New World Cradle of Christmas Tree." *Austin American-Statesman,* December 1, 1954.

Blalock, Fred Frank. "Cowboys' Christmas." *Texas Parade,* December, 1973, pp. 49–51.

Blasig, Anne. *The Wends of Texas.* Brownsville, Tex.: Springman-King Printing, 1974.

Bollaert, William. *William Bollaert's Texas.* Edited by W. Eugene Hollon and Ruth Lapham Butler. Norman: University of Oklahoma Press, 1956.

Bounds, Allene. "Theme of Simple Ballad Is Carried Out at Each Dance." Abilene *Reporter-News,* December 18, 1938.

Bronson, Juli R. "Kwansaa Melds Past, Present." *San Antonio Light,* December, 1981.

Buchner, Edda. "German Christmas." New Braunfels *Herald-Zeitung,* December 25, 1986.

Burton, Gerry. "Candlelight Christmas Tour Recalls Memories." *Lubbock Avalanche-Journal,* November 25, 1979.

Caldwell, Lillie Moerhe. *Texas Wends: Their First Half-Century.* Salado, Texas: Anson Jones Press, 1961.

Callan, Austin. "Rangers Christmas in 1862." *Frontier Times,* December, 1948, pp. 52–54.

Campbell, Harry H. *The Early History of Motley County.* San Antonio: Naylor, 1958.

Carmack, George. "The Cowboys' Christmas Ball." San Antonio *Express-News,* December 25, 1976.

————. "Norwegian Christmas Dinner Is Not the Usual, but Lutefisk." San Antonio *Express-News.* December 14, 1974.

"Carols Add Joy to Season." *Věstník,* December 15, 1982.

Carroll, Curt. "Christmas Heritage." *Texas Parade,* December, 1961.

Carrow, Catherine Ikard. "Amusements for Men and Women in Texas in the 1880's." *West Texas Historical Association Year Book* 23 (October, 1947).

Casey, Betty. *Dance across Texas.* Austin: University of Texas Press, 1985.

Castro Colonies Heritage Association. *Old Favorite Receipts.* Castroville: Castro Colonies Heritage Association, 1977.

Chittenden, Larry. "The Cowboys' Christmas Ball." *Austin American-Statesman,* December 5, 1956.

"Christmas Customs in Czechoslovakia." *Věstník,* December 10, 1980, pp. 17–18.

"Christmas Customs Reflect Diverse Culture." *Texas PTA Magazine,* Dec. 1970, pp. 3–4.

"Christmas Dinner on the Upper Brazos in 1872." *West Texas Historical Association Year Book* 14 (October, 1938): 83.

"Christmas Food with 'Old Country' Flavor." *Věstník,* December 17, 1980, pp. 15–16.

"Christmas in San Antonio." San Antonio *Express-News,* December 26, 1892.

"Christmas in the Confederacy." *Texas Star,* December 19, 1971, p. 6.

"Christmas Lore." *Sky,* December, 1981, pp. 32–36.

"A City of Christmas Tradition." *Magazine of San Antonio,* December, 1978, pp. 57–59.

Clemens, Gus. *The Concho Country.* San Antonio: Mulberry Avenue Books, 1980.

Coffin, Tristram Potter. *The Illustrated Book of Christmas Folklore.* New York: Seabury Press, 1973.

Cohen, Hennig, and Tristram Potter Coffin, eds. *The Folklore of American Holidays*. Detroit, Michigan: Gale Research Co., 1987.

Cominos, Helen. "Greek Christmas Ghosts Scream the Loudest." *Orthodox Observer*, December, 1980, pp. 6–7.

"Congress of the Rounders." *Frontier Times,* October, 1948, pp. 27–28.

Cook, Molly Connor. "Belles of Past Years Recall Gay Holidays." *Austin American-Statesman,* December 23, 1928.

Cope, Millard. "Texas' First Christmas Dates Back to 270 Years Ago." *Austin American-Statesman,* December 25, 1953.

"Cowboys Made Own Early Day Christmases." San Angelo *Standard Times,* December 24, 1954.

Custer, Elizabeth B. *Tenting on the Plains; or, General Custer in Kansas and Texas*. New York: Charles L. Webster and Co., 1887.

Cutrer, Thomas W. *The English Texans*. San Antonio: University of Texas Institute of Texan Cultures, 1985.

"Deep Religious Atmosphere Marked Early-Day Christmas among Few Residents of Texas." San Antonio *Express-News,* December 24, 1930.

Dickens, Charles. *The Pickwick Papers*. New York: Airmont Publishing Co., 1969.

Dobie, J. Frank. *Stories of Christmas and the Bowie Knife*. Austin: Steck Co., 1953.

Domenech, Emmanuel Henri. *Missionary Adventures in Texas and Mexico: A Personal Narrative of Six Years' Sojourn in Those Regions*. London; Longman, Brown, Green, Longmans and Roberts, 1858.

Donecker, Frances. "Christmas in San Antonio Yesterday and Today." *Southern Messenger,* December 21, 1944, pp. 1–3.

Douglas, C. L. "Cattle Kings of Texas." *Cattleman,* December, 1936, pp. 9–13.

Dresel, Gustav. *Gustav Dresel's Houston Journal Adventures in North America and Texas 1837–1841*. Translated and edited by Max Freund. Austin: University of Texas Press, 1954.

Duke, Mrs. R. L. "Christmas on the XIT Ranch." *Cattleman,* December, 1951.

———. "Cowboys' Christmas Dance on the Buffalo Springs XIT Ranch." *Cattleman,* December, 1952, pp. 84–87.

Dworaczyk, Edward J. *The First Polish Colonies of America in Texas.* San Antonio: Naylor Co., 1936.

Dybala, Barbara, and Helen Macik, comps. *Generation to Generation: Czech Foods, Customs and Traditions, Texas Style.* Dallas: Historical Society of the Czech Club, n.d.

Dyer, J. O. "Holiday Season in Early Texas." *Galveston Daily News,* December 26, 1920.

Ehret, Walter, and George K. Evans, comps. *The International Book of Christmas Carols.* Englewood Cliffs, N.J.: Prentice-Hall, 1963.

Elgin, Jack. "Christmas Dinner on the Upper Brazos in 1872." *West Texas Historical Association Year Book* 14 (October, 1938): 83–91.

Emrich, Duncan. "A Certain Nicholas of Patara." *American Heritage,* December, 1960, pp. 22–27.

Erle [Frank Eberle], "A War-Time Christmas in Texas." *Texas Magazine,* December, 1909, p. 42.

Estill, Julia. "Customs among the German Descendants of Gillespie County." *Coffee in the Gourd.* Edited by J. Frank Dobie. Dallas: Southern Methodist University Press, 1923.

———. "Turning Back the Clock." Fredericksburg *Standard,* December 21, 1977.

Fenley, Florence. *Oldtimers of Southwest Texas.* Uvalde, Texas: Hornby Press, 1957.

———. "'Twas the Night before Christmas." *Cattleman,* December, 1941, pp. 5–9.

Fischer, Dora Weiser. *As I Remember.* Kingsville, Texas: Heritage Press, 1983.

Fitz Patrick, Helen. "Keeping Christmas a Joyful Tradition." *Heritage,* November–December, 1978, pp. 2–11.

Foree, Kenneth. "1885 Christmas Feast and Famine." *Dallas Morning News,* December 25, 1951.

———. "When a New Year Meant Champagne." *Dallas Morning News,* January 1, 1952.

Frink, Cheryl Coggins. "Because We Love." *Austin American-Statesman,* December 25, 1987.

Fuermann, George. "The New Year in Houston 1864." Houston: C. Dorman David's the Bookman, 1964. Pamphlet.

Geiser, Samuel Wood. *Naturalists of the Frontier.* Dallas: Southern Methodist University Press, 1948.

Gentry, Diane K. "Sixty-seven Christmases Together." *Modern Maturity,* December, 1982–January, 1983, pp. 39–40.

George, Marjorie. "A Christmas Chronicle." *Southwest Airlines Magazine,* December, 1978, pp. 64–71.

———. "An Old World Christmas." *Southwest Airlines Magazine,* December, 1977, pp. 59–61.

"The German Experience." *Lower Colorado Review* 3 (Second Quarter, 1978): 13–20.

Giddens, Joyce. "O Christmas Tree, O Christmas Tree." *Oasis,* December, 1981, pp. 24–25.

Gilles, John. "Tales of Christmas Past." *Austin American-Statesman,* December, 1981.

Gillett, James B. *Six Years with the Texas Rangers, 1875–1881.* Edited by Milo Milton Quaife. New Haven: Yale University Press, 1925.

Goebel, Nancy. "Spirit of the Wends." *Texas Highways,* February, 1985, pp. 40–47.

Green, Bill. *The Dancing Was Lively: Fort Concho, Texas—A Social History, 1867–1882.* San Angelo: Fort Concho Sketches Publishing Co., 1974.

Greene, A. C. *A Christmas Tree.* Austin: Encino Press, 1973.

———. *The Santa Claus Bank Robbery.* New York: Alfred A. Knopf, 1972.

Grider, Sylvia Ann. *The Wendish Texans.* San Antonio: University of Texas Institute of Texan Cultures, 1982.

Hafertepe, Kenneth. *A History of the French Legation.* Austin: Texas State Historical Association, 1989.

Hale, Leon. "Shooting Anvils Once Great Christmas Sport for Texans." *Houston Post,* December 25, 1962.

Hams, William H. "How Christmas Once Was in West Texas." *Lubbock Avalanche-Journal,* December 17, 1962.

Hart, Katherine. "Early Merchants Compete during Christmas Season." *Austin American-Statesman,* December 5, 1970.

———. "The Eve of Yule in 1863." *Austin American-Statesman,* December 25, 1971.

————. "Fireworks, Cheaper Prices Missed by Holiday Celebrants." *Austin American-Statesman,* December 19, 1970.

————. "Holiday Happenings in Early Day Texas." *Texas Star,* November 12, 1972, p. 2.

————. "How about Nice Solid Gold Toothpicks?" *Austin American-Statesman,* December 7, 1968.

————. "Julia Pease's Christmastime Included Love and Patience." *Austin American-Statesman,* December 18, 1971.

Helm, Mary S. *Scraps of Early Texas History.* Austin: W. M. Morrison, 1985.

"Help the Poor of Austin," *Austin American-Statesman,* December 24, 1895.

Hillert, Patricia. "New Year 100 Years Ago." *San Antonio Light,* January 1, 1950.

Hocker, Emity. "O, Tannenbaum." New Braunfels *Herald-Zeitung,* December 14, 1979.

Hogan, William Ransom. *The Texas Republic: A Social and Economic History.* Norman: University of Oklahoma Press, 1946.

Holder, Judith, and Alison Harding. *Christmas Fare.* Secaucus, N.J.: Chartwell Books, 1981.

"Holiday Celebrations Continue." San Antonio *Express-News,* December 18, 1983.

"Holiday Superstitions." Nassau *Tribune,* December 24, 1980.

Holub, Veronica. "Another Danish Christmas." El Campo *Leader News,* December 22, 1976.

"How Austin Will Spend Christmas." *Austin American-Statesman,* December 21, 1914.

Huber, Leonard V. *Creole Collage.* Lafayette: University of Southwestern Louisiana, 1980.

Hughes, Thomas, ed. *G. T. T.: Gone to Texas; Letters from Our Boys.* London: Macmillan and Co., 1884.

Hugman, Peggy. "Yule of 1880's Springs to Life." New Braunfels *Herald-Zietung,* November 8, 1973.

Hunter, Robert Hancock. *Narrative of Robert Hancock Hunter, 1813–1902.* Edited by B. G. Green. Austin: Cook Printing Co., 1936.

Jackson, Ralph Semmes. *Home on the Double Bayou: Memories of an East Texas Ranch.* Austin: University of Texas Press, 1961.

Jandacek, Marie L. *Czech National Cook Book*. Cicero, Ill.: Western Printing Co., 1956.

Jaques, Mary J. *Texan Ranch Life*. London: Horace Cox, 1894. Reprint. College Station: Texas A&M University Press, 1989.

Jordan, Gilbert J. *Yesterday in the Texas Hill Country*. College Station: Texas A&M University Press, 1979.

Joutel, Henri. *Joutel's Journal of La Salle's Last Voyage,* with notes by Melville B. Anderson. 1896. Reprint. New York: Burt Franklin, 1968.

Kalman, Bobbie. *Early Christmas*. New York: Crabtree Publishing Co., 1981.

Kane, Harnett. *The Southern Christmas Book*. New York: David McKay Co., 1958.

King, Dick. "The Santa Claus Bandit." *Texas Co-op Power,* (December, 1967): 2.

Knopp, Danette. "Frohe Weihnachten!" *Texas Hill Country View,* Holiday–January, 1989.

Kucera, D. "Gingerbread Cookies." *Naši Dějiny,* November–December, 1983.

Kuykendall, J. H. "Reminiscences of Early Texans." *Texas Historical Association Quarterly* 7 (July, 1903): 29–31.

Lake, Mary Daggett. "Pioneer Christmas Customs of Tarrant County." *Publications of the Texas Folk-Lore Society* 5. Edited by J. Frank Dobie. Austin: Texas Folk-Lore Society, 1926, pp. 107–11.

Leckie, Shirley. "Fort Concho: Paradise for Children." *Fort Concho Report* 19 (Spring, 1987): 1–12.

Leman, Mattie W. "San Antonio Belles and Beaux of the Early Fifties." San Antonio *Express-News,* December 25, 1910.

Lich, Glen E. *The German Texans*. San Antonio: University of Texas Institute of Texan Cultures, 1981.

"Lighting the Yule Log." *Austin American-Statesman,* December 18, 1966.

"Lions Community Christmas Program Now Part of Traditional Observance." Fredericksburg *Standard,* December 20, 1967.

Lone Star Gas Co., Home Economics Dept. *Festival of Gas World Cookbook*. Austin: Lone Star Gas Co., n.d.

Love, Katherine McLennan. "German Winter Festivals in Fredericksburg, Texas." *American-German Review,* December, 1949, pp. 17–20.

"Lutefisk Draws Large Crowd." Clifton *Record,* December 6, 1984.

McClintock, William A. "Journal of a Trip through Texas and Northern Mexico in 1846–1847." *Southwestern Historical Quarterly* 34 (January, 1931): 249.

McCracken, Harold. *A Pictorial History of the West.* Garden City, N.Y.: Doubleday and Co., 1966.

Machann, Clinton, and James W. Mendl. *Krásná Amerika: A Study of the Texas Czechs, 1851–1939.* Austin: Eakin Press, 1983.

Macias, George. "Celebrating Christmas in Texas before 1900." *Fayette Electric Co-op Power,* December, 1988, pp. 2–3.

McNeal, Herb. "Texans of 1862 Found Little Christmas Cheer." *Dallas Morning News,* December 23, 1962.

Madison, Virginia Duncan, and Hallie Crawford Stillwell. *How Come It's Called That? Place Names in the Big Bend Country.* Privately printed, 1988.

Maguire, Jack. "Christmas Has Long Been a Texas Tradition." *Austin American-Statesman,* December 24, 1978.

———. "First U.S. Christmas Observed in Texas 1599." Wichita Falls *Times Record News,* December 24 and 25, 1988.

———. "This Is Texas." *Texas Parade,* December, 1972, p. 6.

Males, Mrs. L. L. "Christmas Recollections." *Amarillo Daily News,* December 29, 1965.

Marshall, Bruce. "Christmas in the Confederacy." *El Paso Times,* December 19, 1971.

Martin, Leland. "Area Pioneers Recall Christmases Past." *Midland Reporter-Telegram,* December 21, 1980.

The Melting Pot: Ethnic Cuisine in Texas. San Antonio: University of Texas Institute of Texan Cultures, 1983.

"Memories of Christmas." *Magazine of San Antonio,* December, 1977, pp. 43–51.

Miller, Ray. "Christmas in Texas." *AAA World,* November–December, 1988, p. 2b.

Morfi, Juan Agustín de. *Excerpts from the Memorias for the History of the Province of Texas.* San Antonio: Naylor Printing Co., 1932.

Mosebach, Fred. "Mission of Maennerchor Asserts Itself at Christmas Time." San Antonio *Express-News,* December 20, 1936.

Naylor, June G. "Christmas in Texas." *Fort Worth Star-Telegram,* November 22, 1987.

Noonan-Guerra, Mary Ann. "A City of Christmas Tradition." *Magazine of San Antonio,* December, 1979, pp. 49–54.

"Old Timers Recall Christmas of 90's." *Austin American-Statesman,* December 25, 1930.

"Old World Traditions Still Observed in U.S." *San Antonio Light,* December 24, 1978.

Olmsted, Frederick Law. *A Journey through Texas: Saddle-Trip on the Southwestern Frontier.* New York: Burt Franklin, 1969.

Ol' Waddy. "Boyhood Christmas on the Staked Plains." *Western Horseman,* December, 1962.

Owens, William A. *Tell Me a Story, Sing Me a Song: A Texas Chronicle.* Austin: University of Texas Press, 1983.

Parvin, Bob. "Texas Christmases Past." *Texas Highways,* (December, 1973), pp. 2–7.

Pazdral, Olga. "Some Czech Christmas Traditions and Superstitions." *Naše Dějiny* (Hallettsville, Tex.), November–December, 1983.

Petmecky, William. "Gillespie Cedars First Texas Yule Trees." *Austin American-Statesman,* December 23, 1954.

Pinkard, Tommie. "Christmas in San Antonio." *Texas Highways,* December, 1977, p. 4.

Polanie Club. *The Polish Christmas Story.* New York: Kosciuszko Foundation, 1971.

Pope, Harold C. "Christmas at Old Fort Concho." *True West,* December, 1983, pp. 32–35.

Ramsdell, Charles. "Former Christmases in the Southwest." San Antonio *Express-News,* December 21, 1947.

Rapp, Mrs. I. H. "Los Pastores Is Gem of Miracle Plays." *El Palacio* (Santa Fe) 11 (December, 1921): 151–63.

Rawick, George P., ed. *The American Slave: A Composite Autobiography.* Ser. 2, vols. 2–10, *Texas Narratives.* Westport, Conn.: Greenwood Publishing Co., 1972–73.

Reeves, Frank. "Anson Makes Annual Event of the Cowboys' Christmas Ball." *Cattleman,* December, 1938, p. 25.

Roemer, Ferdinand. *Texas: With Particular Reference to German Immigra-*

tion. Translated by Oswald Mueller. San Antonio: Standard Printing, 1935.

Ross, Mary Fisk. "Woman Recalls Early Christmas." San Antonio *Express-News*, December 24, 1933.

Rutter, Patricia Skarry. "Louis Prang's Christmas Card Masterpieces." *Ford Times*, December, 1978, pp. 11–17.

Saint Mary's Church. *Christmas Carols and Polish Koledy*. Panna Maria, Texas: Saint Mary's Church, n.d. Booklet.

"Santa, Counterparts Awaited Everywhere." *San Antonio Light*, December 24, 1978.

Schmitt, Martin F. "Frontier Army Christmas." *Cattleman*, December, 1944.

Schreiber, William I. "The First American Christmas Tree." *American-German Review*, December, 1943, pp. 4–5.

Schutze, Alvina. "One of the First Christmas Trees in Austin." *Austin Homes and Gardens*, December, 1981, pp. 29–31.

Scobee, B. *Fort Davis, Texas, 1583–1960*. El Paso, Tex.: Hill Printing Co., 1963.

Scott, Irene. "Christmas Cow Customs." *Cattleman*, December, 1952, pp. 115–16.

Seele, Hermann. *The Cypress and Other Writings of a German Pioneer in Texas*. Translated by Edward C. Breitenkamp. Austin: University of Texas Press, 1979.

Shuffler, Henderson. "'Dixie' Becomes a Yule Song." *Houston Chronicle*, December 24, 1973.

———. "Pioneer Celebrations Rambunctious – But Human." Goliad Texas *Express*, December 22, 1963.

Silverthorne, Elizabeth. *Plantation Life in Texas*. College Station: Texas A&M University Press, 1986.

Simmons, Lee. "Observations on Horses across Seventy-five Years." *Southwestern Historical Quarterly* 58 (October, 1954): 210–13.

Skrabanek, Robert L. *We're Czechs*. College Station: Texas A&M University Press, 1988.

Snyder, Phillip. "Christmas Tree Ornaments." *Americana*, November, 1976, pp. 26–29.

Sokolnicki, Alfred J. "Celebrating a Traditional Polish Christmas." *European World-USA*, December–January, 1981, pp. 1–3.

Sorensen, Sydney Scout. "The Wends of Texas." Goliad Texas *Express,* July 17, 1949.

"Star Shines on El Paso Mountainside." *Laredo Morning Times,* December 19, 1987.

Sterne, Adolphus. "Diary of Adolphus Sterne." Edited by Harriet Smither. *Southwestern Historical Quarterly* 35 (July, 1931).

———. *Hurrah for Texas! The Diary of Adolphus Sterne, 1838–1851.* Edited by Archie P. McDonald. Waco, Tex.: Texian Press, 1969.

Strybel, Robert. "Making Christmas '83 – Polish, Joyous and Meaningful." *Narod Polski,* December 8, 1983.

Stumpf, Ella K. Daggett. "Christmas in Old San Antonio." *Magazine of San Antonio,* December, 1977, pp. 62–68.

———. "Spirits of Christmas Past." *Magazine of San Antonio,* December, 1977, pp. 52–56.

Taylor, Margie. "Wartime Yule." *San Antonio Light,* December 6, 1957.

"Texas Christmas Past." *Texas Highways,* December, 1973, p. 2.

"Texas Plants in Christmas Legends." *Cattleman,* December, 1956, pp. 57–58.

"This Is Texas – Early Holiday." *Texas Parade,* December, 1973, 4.

"This Is Texas – First Christmas." *Texas Parade,* December, 1968, 4.

"This Is Texas – Traditions That Live." *Texas Parade,* December, 1972, 6.

Timmermann Sisters. "Keeping Christmas." *Texas Library Journal,* December, 1935, 117–23.

Tolbert, Frank X. "Lutefisk Arrives in Cranfills Gaps." *Dallas Morning News,* December 3, 1970.

Tolman, J. C. "Christmas 1866 and Mount Bonnell." *Texaco Star,* December, 1924, 9–22.

———. "Christmas 1887 in Palo Duro Canyon." *Texaco Star,* December, 1925, 16–22.

Toudouze, Susan. "Christmas Means Family Tradition." *North San Antonio Times,* December, 1972.

Trenckmann, William. *A Christmas in Troubled Times.* Round Top, Texas: Friends of Winedale, 1976.

Vielé, Teresa Griffin. *Following the Drum: A Glimpse of Frontier Life.* Lincoln: University of Nebraska Press, 1984.

Vogel, Victor. "Wendish Christmas," *Free and Easy.* Clipping in Wendish Heritage Museum Archives.

Walsh, Francis J. "My Dear Let Me Explain about Mistletoe." *Smithsonian,* December, 1974, 116.

Walther, Gary. "The German Tree in America." *American History,* December, 1982, 15–17.

Watson, Ann Maria. "Tales of Christmas Past." *Magazine of San Antonio,* December, 1978, 57–59.

Watson, C. J. "Two Christmas Trees Which Made History." *Dallas Morning News,* December 18, 1932.

Webb, Walter Prescott. "Christmas and New Year in Texas." *Southwestern Historical Quarterly* 44 (January, 1941): 357–79.

Williams, R. H. *With the Border Ruffians: Memories of the Far West, 1852–1868.* Edited by E. W. Williams. New York: E. P. Dutton and Co., 1907.

Wolff, Henry, Jr. "Christmas and Early Texans." Victoria *Advocate,* December 15, 1985.

Wrightman, Marj. "Woodlawn Yule Brightens Civil War." *Austin American-Statesman,* December 18, 1963.

Young, Kevin. "Facts and Footnotes." Goliad Texas *Express,* December 11, 1985.

Illustration Credits

Page x: "A Happy Hanukah," postmarked 1940.

Page 2: "Just a little line to say . . ."

Page 10: "Ring Christmas peace . . . ," postmarked 1909.

Page 20: Our Lady of Guadalupe. Courtesy Lydia Santiago, Temple, Texas.

Page 32: Poinsettia, holly, and pinecones, postmarked 1916.

Page 47: Elves with tree and wheelbarrow, reproductions of turn-of-the-century die-cut cards.

Page 50: 1988 Christmas card, drawing of Nigerian crèche figures by Doris Hiebert, Bryan, Texas.

Page 55: *Top,* "Santa's Special." *Bottom,* "Santa Claus Express."

Page 58: "Fröhliche Weihnachten," postmarked 1909. Courtesy Charlotte Andre, Salado, Texas.

Page 63: "Prosit!" postmarked 1904(?). Courtesy Charlotte Andre, Salado, Texas.

Page 71: "New Year Greetings."

Page 76: Snowy street scene, "Christmas Greetings . . ."

Page 79: "A Joyful Christmas," postmarked 1931.

Page 92: "Jesu Christ was born.
We will buy him a leather coat
Very long and furry
So he would have it to his heels."
Courtesy SPJST Museum, Temple, Texas.

Page 101: "A hearty wish . . . ," postmarked 1911.

Page 103: Santa with children, reproduction of turn-of-the-century die-cut card.

Page 106: "Glaedelig Jul," from *Norseman* 6, November, 1985. Courtesy Solveig Herndon, Arlington, Texas.

Page 112: "Wishing you a Happy Christmas."

Page 116: Children, reproduction of turn-of-the-century die-cut card.

Page 125: *Top*, "Xmas Limited." *Bottom*, "To wish you a happy New Year," postmarked 1910.

Page 128: Canal scene.

Page 134: Elf with tree, reproduction of turn-of-the-century die-cut card.

Page 144: Woodcut, "Silent Night, Holy Night," by Martin Nowak. Courtesy Wendish Heritage Museum Archives, Serbin Texas.

Page 150: Icon Christmas card. Courtesy Evangelos and Susan Pepps, Waco, Texas.

Color Plates

Following page 66:

Santa in blue suit, postmarked 1910.

Children ringing bells. Courtesy Mary El-Beheri, San Antonio, Texas.

Two wise men, "May Peace and Christmas . . . ," dated 1925.

Santa on donkey.

Three wise men, "Joyful Christmas Greetings . . . ," dated 1924.

Man cutting tree for two girls. Courtesy SPJST Museum, Temple, Texas.

Church in the snow, "A Merry Christmas."

Snow scene with children. Courtesy SPJST Museum, Temple, Texas.

"I wish you a Merry Xmas," dated 1909.

Following page 98:

Santa with walking stick and bag.

Bird on holly, postmarked 1910.

Nativity scene with shepherds, dated 1922.

Mary and child.

Mary on donkey, postmarked 1933. Courtesy Charlotte Andre, Salado, Texas.

Sheep and hourglasses.

"May these wishes . . ."

"Best Wishes for Christmas," postmarked 1910.

Bell, holly, and sash, postmarked 1924.

Index

Adam, Adolphe Charles, 122
Adelsverein, 59
"Adeste Fideles," 90
Advent calendar, 162n.5
Advent wreath, 64–65
Aeblekage (recipe), 111
Alamo, the, 21–22, 31
Alarcón, Martín de, 51
Alsace (France), 120
Alsatian New Year's Bread (recipe), 124
Alsatians, 118
Amahl and the Night Visitors, 131
American Poinsettia Society, 22–23
Andersen, Hans Christian, 110
"Angels o'er the Fields Were Singing," 122
animals, 108, 146
anise cookies, 72
annexation, 9
Anson, Tex., xi, 37–39
antebellum statehood, 9–12
aquavit, 114
"Auld Land Syne," 90–91
Austin, Stephen F., 5, 6, 7
Austin, Tex.: and Christmas celebrations, 15, 17–18; and French Legation, 118–19; and New Year's receptions, 16; during Reconstruction, 13–14
Avgolemono (recipe), 153

Bach's "Christmas Oratorio," 68
Baklava (recipe), 154
balls, 37, 52. *See also* dancing
Barker, S. Omar, 16
Barnfest, 109–10
"Barn Jesus," 110
Bastrop, Baron de, 4
Beethoven Männerchor, 17, 67

"Behold That Star," 53
Bengal fire, 119, 163n.5
Bernardi, Prospero, 129
beseda, 102–104
Bethany Congregational Church, San Antonio, 67
Bethlehem, Tex., 5
Big Brothers program, 17
birds, 108–109
Biscuit *Tortoni* (recipe), 133
Bishop of Myra. *See* Saint Nicholas
Black Peter, x
Blessing of the Animals, 21
Boar's Head Festival, 88–90
Bollaert, William, 37, 39, 52, 88
"Born Was Christ the Lord," 95
Braehead Ranch, 90
Bray, Esther L., 73, 74, 97, 98
Brooks, Phillips, 46
Brownsville, Tex., 119
buche de Noël, 123
Buñuelos (recipe), 29
Burell, Jimmy, 124
Burns, Robert, 85, 90
Buttermilk Pie (recipe), 48

Cabeza de Vaca, Álvar Núñez, 51
Café Brûlot (recipe), 124, 126
Cajuns, 121, 122, 123
Cake of the King, 127
Campbell, Henry, 42–43
Campbell, Lizzie, 42–43
"Campbells Are Coming, The," 37
Canary Islanders, 160n.2
candles, 109, 110; in Advent wreath, 64–65; religious service using, 67; symbolism of, 81–82

candy pulling, 39
cards, Christmas, 69, 82
carols: American composers of, 46–47; British, 90–91; Czech, 94–95; Danish, 109; French, 122–23; German, 67–68; Italian, 131; Orthodox, 151; Polish, 140–41; Wendish, 147. *See also* music; spirituals; *individual titles*
"Carol of the Bagpipers, The," 131
"Carol of the Birds," 122
"Carols of the Flowers," 122
Castro, Henri, 118
Castroville, Tex., 118, 119
Castroville *Parisa* (recipe), 124
ceppo, 133
cesnica, 155
champurrado, 29
Chicago's Century of Progress, 38
Chicken and Sausage Gumbo (recipe), 126
"Children Go Where I Send Thee," 54
Children's Toys throughout the Ages, 69
Chinese Lunar New Year, ix
Chittenden, Larry, 37–38
Christkindlein, 65
Christmas at Old Fort Concho, 45–46
"Christmas at the French Legation," 123
Christmas Carol, A, 90–91
"Christmas Cradle Hymn," 140
Christmas Creek, 5
Christmas Mountains, 5
Christmas trees: community, 17, 39–40, 59; Czech, 98–99; English, 80; evolution of, 7, 10–11, 14, 15–16, 120; feather, 62; French, 120–21; German, 60, 61, 62–64, 69; Italian, 133; Paradise, 62; on plantations, 51; Polish, 138; Scandinavian, 109–10; Timmermann, 60–61; Wendish, 147–48. *See also* decorations
Christopher Columbus Society of San Antonio, 129
circuses, 14–15
Cisco, Tex., 18
Civil War, 12–13
Coffee Cake (recipe), 149
Coffee in the Gourd, 65–66
Columbus, Christopher, 129
"Come, Hear the Wonderful Tidings," 95

Cominos, Helen, 152
commercialization of holidays, 18–19
confetti carnivals, 11
Congress of the Rounders, 8
Conservation Society of San Antonio, 26
cookie cutters, 70
cookies. *See* recipes; *individual names*
"Cop and the Anthem, The," 48
Coppini, Pompeo, 129
Corn Bread (recipe), 56
Corpus Christi, Tex., 18
Cowboys' Christmas Ball, xi
"Cowboys' Christmas Ball, The," 37–39
Cranfills Gap, Tex., xi, 113–14
crèche, 121. *See also nacimiento;* Nativity scene; *presepio*
Cushing, Edward H., 69
Custer, Elizabeth, 13–14
Custer, George Armstrong, 13–14
Czech Christmas Bread (recipe), 98, 99
Czech immigration, 93

dahke, 155
Daiken, Leslie, 69
Dallas, Tex., 16, 38
Dallas Czech Singers, 94
Damenchor, 68
dances: as events, 11, 36, 37, 39, 52, 122, 160n.6; types of, 27, 36–37, 38, 39, 53, 68, 90, 102, 109, 122, 155, 160n.6. *See also individual dances*
dancing, 34, 39–41, 44, 68, 78, 102, 104, 122, 155; prohibition of, 39; on ranches, 43; by slaves, 52–53. *See also* music
Danevang, Tex., 108, 109
Danish Apple Cake (recipe), 111
Davis, Claudia, 40
Day of the Oak, 154
"Deck the Halls," 90
decorations, 10–11; African-American, 56–57; Czech, 99; French, 120–21; German, 69; Italian, 133; Polish, 138; Scandinavian, 109; straw as, 108, 155; on Timmermann tree, 60–61; Victorian, 80. *See also* Christmas trees
"Der Christbaum ist der Schoenste Baum," 147
D'Hanis, Tex., 123

Dickens, Charles, 77, 87
Dickens on the Strand, xi, 77
"Dixie," 14
Dobie, J. Frank, 43
dolmathes, 153
Domenech, Abbé Henri, 119–20
"Dormi, Dormi, O Bel Bambino," 131
Dresel, Gustav, 59
drinking, 40, 59–60, 77, 117; Czech tradi-
    tions of, 101; in Republic, 7, 8–9, 34,
    59–60; Scandinavian traditions of,
    114. See also *individual drinks*
Dwight, John, 122
Dyer, J. O., 117

egg hunt, Christmas, 78
eggnog, 7, 11, 15, 88
Egg-Nog Branch, 5
eggs, 7, 138–39
Elgin, Jack, 35–36
El Paso, Tex., 18
English immigration, 78
Epiphany, 126, 130, 163n.1. See also Magi;
    Three Kings; Three Wise Men, Day
    of the
Ervendberg, Rev. Louis C., 59, 61
Ervendberg Orphanage, 61–62
Estevan (Stephen the Moor), 51
Estill, Julia, 65–66

fais-dodo, 122
Fannin, Jr., James W., 6
farolitos, 160n.5
Father Christmas, 66, 77, 82
Father Ice, x
Feast of Lights, ix
Feast of the Immaculate Conception,
    94
Feast of the Kings, 126
feather trees, 62
Festival of Lights, 24–25
Festival of the Stars, 135
Filisola, Gen. Vicente, 129
fireworks, 15, 18, 31, 33, 41, 120; in Czech
    superstition, 100; danger of, 35; on
    Jaques Ranch, 84; on plantations,
    40. See also noisemaking
"First Nowell, The," 90
Folklife Festival, 123
folklore. See fortunetelling; superstitions;
    weather forecasting

food, 10, 35–36, 61–62, 121–23; Anglo-
    American, 48; British, 77, 83–86, 87;
    Cajun, 121, 123; Czech, 95–99, 101,
    104, 162n.6; German, 69; Italian, 131–
    33; on plantations, 40, 52, 54, 56; Pol-
    ish, 138, 142; on ranches, 42–44;
    Scandinavian, 111–15; Wendish, 147–
    48. See also recipes; *individual dishes*
Fort Concho, 44–46
Fort Davis, 44
forts: Christmas at, 44–46
fortunetelling: Czech, 99–100, 104;
    French, 124; Polish, 137, 142. See also
    superstitions
Fort Worth, Tex., 88–89
Frazier, John, 40–41
Fredericksburg, Tex., xi, 66–67, 68
French explorers, 3
French Legation, 118–19, 123
"From Starry Skies Thou Cometh," 131
Frost Man, 136
"Frosty the Snowman," 48
fruitcake, 74, 85, 147

Galveston, Tex., xi, 9, 77, 78, 117, 146
games, 39, 82–84, 102. See also fortune-
    telling
geographical holiday names, 5
german (dance), 36, 122, 160n.6
German immigration, 59
Geronimo, Tex., 60
ghosts, Christmas, 91, 152
Giddings, Tex., 145
gift giving, 21, 40, 41, 49, 61, 69; African-
    American, 57; in antebellum period,
    10; in Civil War period, 13–14; Chi-
    nese, ix; Czech, 94, 99; Greek, 152;
    Italian, 130; on plantations, 51–52;
    Polish, 136, 140; on ranches, 42–43;
    Swedish, 109; Wendish, 148, 149
"Gift of the Magi, The," 48
Giles, Alfred, 89–90
Gillett, Jim, 36
Gingerbread Men (recipe), 98
"God Rest Ye Merry, Gentlemen," 90
Golden Legend, x
golden pig, 97–98
"Good King Wenceslas," 95
Goodnight (JA) Ranch, 42
goose, 72, 147
"Go Tell It on the Mountain," 53

"Gott ist die Liebe," 147
Governor's Mansion, Austin, 151
glocken, xi
"Glory to God in the Highest," 75
Greek Revival Architecture, 151–52
Greene, A. C., 18
"Greensleeves," 90
Grierson, Benjamin Henry, 45
"Grinder's Polka," 102
Gruene, Tex., 62
Guinagato Ranche, 83
gunpowder. *See* noisemaking

haggis, 85
Handel's *Messiah*, 68
Hanukkah, ix, 17
"Happiness Waltz," 102
Henry, O., 48
Henry VIII, 87
Henry VII, 87, 115
herring, 114
"Herr Schmitt," 122
Hillingdon Ranch, 89–90
Hogmanay, 84–85
Holley, Mary Austin, 7–8
holly, 80, 81
"Home, Sweet Home," 44
Honey Cake (recipe), 140
Hord, Thomas A., 9
Houston, Sam, 6, 7, 11, 118
Houston, Tex., 37, 151
Hughes, William, 83
Huntsville, Tex., 39, 52
"Hymn of St. Nicholas," 151
hymns. See *individual titles*

"I Heard the Bells on Christmas Day,"
    46–47
"Il Est Né, le Divin Enfant," 122
Indians, 3–4, 5, 21
Institute of Texan Cultures, 60
International Holiday Festival, 133
Irish Coffee (recipe), 86–87
Irish immigration, 78
Italian immigration, 129
"It Came upon the Midnight Clear," 48
ivy, 80

Jackson, Ralph Semmes, 41–42, 79–80
Jackson Ranch, 79–80
Janelli, Adam, 130

Jaques, Mary J., 83–84
Jefferson, Tex., 151
"Jesus, the New-Born Baby," 131
Jewish holiday customs, ix
"Jingle Bells," 48, 123
Johnson (Lyndon Baines) family, 72
Jones, Morgan, 78
Jordan, Gilbert, 70
Joutel's Journal of La Salle's Last Voyage, 3
"Joy to the World," 90
juba, 53
Julatta, 109
julebord, 114
Jule-Nissen, 108
Junction, Tex., 83–84

kallikantzaree, 152
Karankawa Indians, 5
Karenga, Maulana, 57
kibbee, 155
Kilgore, Tex., 18
Kilian, Johann, 146, 147
Kinderfest, 66
King, Henrietta, 43
King Ranch, 43
Knecht Ruprecht, x, 145. *See also*
    Rumpliche
Kolache (recipe), 95–97
koledy, 140
Kris Kringle, 65–67
Kristkindl Market, 66–67
Kwanza, 56–57

La Befána, 130–31
Lafitte, Jean, 51, 117, 163n.1
La Fiesta de las Luminarias, 24–25
L'Alliance Française, 118
La Salle, René Cavelier, Sieur de, 3, 118
Las Posadas, xi, 23–24, 160n.2
Leakey, Tex., 40
Lebanese traditions, 155
Lebkuchen (recipe), 72, 73
Leche Quemada (recipe), 29–30
Lee, Robert E., 11
Lemon Soup (recipe), 153
lichtstock, 62, 133
Livingston, Jr., Henry, 161n.20
Long, Jane, 5
Longfellow, Henry Wadsworth, 46–47
"Looking for My Sweetheart Waltz,"
    102

"Lord Has Sent Redemption, The," 151
Los Pastores, xi, 26–28
Lucas, Anthony Francis, 153, 154
Lucchese, Josephine, 129
luminarias, 18, 25, 160n.5
Lunar New Year, ix
Lundberg (Charles) family, 17
Lutefisk Festival, xi, 113–14
Luther, Martin, 65

Magi, 133. *See also* Three Kings; Three Wise Men, Day of the
manger. *See* crèche; *nacimiento;* Nativity scene; *presepio*
Männerchor, 68
Margil, Fr. Antonio, 21–22
"Mary Had a Baby," 53
marzipan, 72–73
masque balls, 11
matachinas dances, 4, 27
Matador Ranch, 42–43
Matagorda, Tex., 5
Matíčka, 94
Maverick, Mary, 12
Medina, Tex., 34
Menardville, Tex., 36
Mendoza, Juan Domínguez de, 3
menorah, ix
Menotti, Gian Carlo, 131
Merritt, Col. Wesley, 44–45
Meusebach, John O., 62
Mexican rule, 4–6
midnight mass, 30, 121
mince pie, 87, 88
Misa de Gallo, 30
Mission, Tex., 22–23
Mission Garden Club, 23
Mission San Antonio de Valero, 21–22, 31
Mission San José, San Antonio, 21, 26, 28
mistletoe, 65, 80–81, 110
Mkeka, 57
Moczygemba, Fr. Leopold, 135, 142–43
Moerby, Milton, 145
Mole de Guajolote (recipe), 28
"Money Musk," 37
Monnoye, Bernard de la, 122
Montgomery, Tex., 59
Moore, Clement, 46, 161n.20
Muhindi, 57

music, 8, 36, 43; African-American, 53–54; Arabic, 155; British, 90–91; Czech, 94–95, 102; Danish, 109; German, 67–69; Italian, 131. *See also* carols; dancing; spirituals; *individual titles*

nacimiento, 25–26
Nacogdoches, Tex., 34, 37
Nast, Thomas, 46
National Folk Festival (Washington, D.C.), 38
Nativity scene, 130, 141–42. *See also* crèche; *nacimiento, presepio*
New Sweden, Tex., 108, 110
New Wied (Gruene), Tex., 62
New Year Creek, 5
New Year's bread, 123
New Year's celebrations, 8, 30–31, 34, 48, 153; African-American, 57; Chinese, ix, Czech, 102–104; Polish, 142; Scottish, 84–85; Wendish, 148
New Year's receptions, 16
nguzo saba, 56
noisemaking, 9, 11, 33–34, 43, 60, 100, 110. *See also* fireworks
noodles, Wendish (recipe), 148
Norse, Tex., 108
"Now We Have Christmas Again," 109

Obendorf (Austria), 67–68
"O Come All Ye Faithful," 147
"O Holy Night," 122
Old Three Hundred, 5
"Oldtime Christmas Gallyhoot," 16
Olmsted, Frederick L., 34–35
"O Lord, O My Lord, O Lord," 53
Oñate, Juan de, 3
oplatki, 137
"O Po' Little Jesus," 53
ornaments. *See* Christmas trees; decorations
Orthodox Church, 151
"O Tannenbaum," 68
Our Lady of Guadalupe Church, San Antonio, 26
Owens, William, 39

Palm, Svante, 107
Pancho Claus, 21
panettone, 132

Panna Maria, Tex., 135–36, 141, 142–43
Paradise tree, 62
parisa: 123; recipe for, 124
Parker, Daniel, 5–6
pasta, 132
Pasterka, 141
"Pat-a-Pan," 122–23
Pease, Julia, 13
Pease, Lucadia, 12–13, 16, 52
Pebbernodder (recipe), 113
Pecan Pie (recipe), 49
Pelznickel (Furry Nicholas), x
Pepps, Susan, 153
Père Noël, 121
pfeffernuesse: 72, 147; recipe for, 74
Pickwick Papers, The, 77
piernik, 136
Pierogi (recipe), 139
piñatas, 21, 24
plantations, 40–41, 51–52, 88
play parties, 39
Plum Pudding (recipe), 88–89
podlaznik, 138
Poinsett, Joel R., 22
poinsettia, 22–23
polka, 37, 38, 68, 102, 122
"Pop Goes the Weasel," 37
Port Arthur, Tex., 133
Port Lavaca, Tex., 59
posole, 28
Potica (recipe), 156
Prang, Louis, 69, 162n.9
Prang and Company, 82
pranks, 9, 117. *See also* vandalism
presents. *See* gift giving
presepio, 129, 130, 133
puddings, 87
"Put Your Little Foot," 122

Queen of Vietnamese Martyrs Catholic
　Church, Port Arthur, 18
Quintana, Tex., 34

railroads, 15
ranches, 41–44; Braehead, 90; Good-
　night (JA), 42; Guinagato, 83; Hilling-
　don, 89–90; Jackson, 79–80; SMS,
　107; White, 41–42
recipes: *Aeblekage,* 111; Alsatian New Year's
　Bread, 124; *Avgolemono,* 153; Baklava,
　154; Basic Kolache, 96–97; Biscuit *Tor-*

toni, 133; *Buñuelos,* 29; Buttermilk Pie,
　48; Café Brûlot, 126; Castroville *Parisa,*
　124; Chicken and Sausage Gumbo,
　126; Christmas Bread, 99; Corn
　Bread, 56; Gingerbread Men, 98;
　Honey Cake, 140; *Lebkuchen,* 73;
　Leche Quemada, 30; *Mole de Guajolote,*
　28; *Pebbernodder,* 113; *Pfeffernuesse,* 74;
　Pierogi, 139; Plum Pudding, 89; *Potica,*
　156; *Saltimbocca,* 132; *Sandbakkels,* 114;
　Shortbread, 86; Southern Pecan Pie,
　49; Sweet Potato Pone, 54; Tea
　Scones, 85; Timmermann Sisters'
　Christmas Cookies, 70; Welsh Rare-
　bit, 86; Wendish Coffee Cake, 149;
　Wendish Noodles, 148; *Zabaglione,*
　132
Reconstruction Period, 13–14
"Red Wine and White Kolache Polka,"
　102
religious services, 15, 45, 74–75, 119–20;
　Czech, 100; Italian, 130; Norse, 109;
　Orthodox, 151, 156–57; Wendish, 147;
　Yugoslavian, 155
Republic of Texas, 6–9
reveillon, 121
ring dances, 90, 109
Rio Grande, 3
"Rise Up, Shepherd, and Follow," 53
"Rocking Carol, The," 95
rodkal, 114
Roemer, Ferdinand, 9, 60
"Roll Out the Barrel Polka," 102
Rosh Hashanah, ix
"Rudolph the Red-nosed Reindeer," 48,
　93
Ru Klaus (Rough Nicholas), x
Rumpliche, 145, 146, 148

Saengerfests, 68
Saint Basil, 164n.2
Saint Basil's Day, 152–53
Saint Francis of Assisi, 130
Saint Lucia Day, 107
Saint Nicholas traditions: x, 62; British,
　82; Czech, 94, 99; Dutch, 46; French,
　121; German, 65–67; Orthodox, 156–
　57; Polish, 136; Wendish, 145. *See also*
　Father Christmas; Rumpliche; Santa
　Claus
Saint Nicholas Day, 65, 94, 136

Saint Nicholas Orthodox Church, Waco, 156–57
Saint Paul Lutheran Church, Serbin, 146
Saints Constantine and Helen Serbian Orthodox Church, Galveston, 154
Saint Stephen's Day, 101–102, 142
Saint Sylvester's Day, 142
Saint Wenceslas, 95
Salcedo, Gov. Manuel María de, 4
Saligny, Alphonse de, 118
saloons: in Austin, 15
Saltimbocca (recipe), 132
Salvation Army, 17
San Angelo, Tex., xi, 45
San Antonio, Tex., xi, 4, 14–17, 21, 25, 30–31, 51, 57; Folklife Festival in, 123; German music performances in, 68; and Las Posadas, 23–24; and Los Pastores, 26–27
San Antonio Conservation Society, 23
San Augustine, Tex., 37, 151
Sandbakkels (recipe), 114–15
San Fernando Cathedral, San Antonio, 17
Santa Claus, x–xi, 7, 78, 109, 121, 149; in Czech tradition, 94, 99; evolution of, 46; and fiends, x–xi, 145. *See also* Saint Nicholas
Santa Claus Bank Robbery, The, 18
"Santa Claus Is Coming to Town," 48
Scandinavian immigration, 107–108
Schott, Molly Hans, 124
schottische, 37, 38, 122
Scones (recipe), 85
Scott, Sir Walter, 87
Scottish immigration, 78
seals, Christmas, 110
Sears, Edmund, 48
Seaton Choral Club, SPJST Lodge 47, 94–95
Second Christmas, 68
Seele, Hermann, 61–62, 74, 161–62n.3
Serbin, Tex., 146–47
Sharpe, Mrs. H. H., 88–89
Shavano legend, 22
Shepherd's Mass, 135, 141
Shortbread (recipe), 85–86
Shuffler, Henderson, 19
"Silent Night," 67, 95
Silesia (Poland), 135, 142
Siringo, Charles A., 129

SMS ranches, 107
Snap parties, 39
Solms-Braunfels, Prince Carl, 59
Southern Pecan Pie (recipe), 49
Spanish explorers, 3
Spanish Governor's Palace, San Antonio, 4
Spanish rule, 3–4
Spindletop, 153
spirituals, 53–54. *See also* carols
Star Bearer, 135
Sterne, Adolphus, 37
straw, 108, 155
Sundblom, Haddon, 46
superstitions: British, 91; Czech, 94, 97, 99–100, 104; French, 124; Greek, 152; Norwegian, 109; Polish, 137, 142; Scandinavian, 108, 110
sursild, 114
"Sweet Bunch of Daisies," 122
Sweet Potato Pone (recipe), 54
Swenson, Swen Magnus, 107, 108
Swiss customs, ix
syllabub, 88
Syrian customs, 155

tamales, 28
Tannenbaum, 64
tarot cards, 102
Tate, Nahum, 90
Taylor, Charles, 34
Tea Scones (recipe), 85
Terrell, Geraldine, 54
Texas Cowboy, A, 129
Texas Rangers, 35–36
Texas Wendish Heritage Society, 146
"There's a Song in the Air," 48
Three Kings, xi, 21, 26, 94, 104, 142
Three Wise Men, Day of the, 104, 130, 131. *See also* Three Kings
Timmermann family, 60–61, 70, 161–62n.3
Timmermann Sisters' Christmas Cookies (recipe), 70–71
tomte, 108
Tortoni (recipe), 133
tournaments, 82–83
Tower of the Americas, 31
Travis, William Barret, 6
trifle, 85
Tropical Christmas Poinsettia Show, 23
turkey shoots, 15, 35

turon, 141
" 'Twas the Night before Christmas," 46, 93, 161n.20
Twelfth Night, 127
Twelve Days of Christmas, 78–79
"Twelve Nights of a Capital Christmas," 78

Unsen, son of, 3
"Up on the Housetop," 48
Urn of Fate, 130
Ursuline Convent, San Antonio, 23

vandalism, 34–35
Van Zandt, Isaac, 118
Velasco, Tex., 78
Vespucci, Amerigo, 129
Victorian Christmas, 77, 80

Wade, J. F., 90
waltz, 37, 68, 102, 122
Washington County, 11
Washington-on-the-Brazos, Tex., 6
wassail, 87–88, 115
Watt, Isaac, 90
"We Are Going to the Stable," 95
weather forecasting, 94, 104. *See also* superstitions
weddings, 40
Weidmann, August, 73–74

weihnachtsfeier, 67
weihnachtsmann, 66
Weihnachtsstollen, 72
Welsh immigration, 78
Welsh Rarebit (recipe), 86
Wendish Heritage Society, xiii, 148
"We Three Kings of Orient Are," 46
"We Wish You a Merry Christmas," 90
"We Won't Go Home 'Till Morning," 34
"What Child is This?" 90
"While Shepherds Watched Their Flocks by Night," 90
"Whistling Dick's Christmas Stocking," 48
"White Christmas," 48
White Mound, 37
White's Ranch, 41–42
Wigilia, 135, 137, 142

XIT Ranch, 43–44

"Yankee Doodle," 14
"Your Birth O Christ," 151
Yugoslavian customs, 154
Yule, evolution of term, 108
Yule log, 51, 79–80, 108, 154

Zabaglione (recipe), 132
Zilker Park, Austin, 80

Christmas in Texas was composed into type on a Compugraphic digital phototypesetter in eleven point Galliard with three points of spacing between the lines. Galliard Italic was selected for display. The book was designed by Jim Billingsley, typeset by Metricomp, Inc., printed offset by Hart Graphics, Inc., and bound by John H. Dekker & Sons, Inc. The paper on which this book is printed carries acid-free characteristics for an effective life of at least three hundred years.

TEXAS A&M UNIVERSITY PRESS : COLLEGE STATION